BLOODLINES

Books by L. C. Phillips

THE DREAM WINNERS
A Novel

SISTINE CARTOONS
Poems

BLOODLINES
Poems

Bloodlines

by

L. C. PHILLIPS

PULSE-|INGER

Standard Book Number 0-912282-02-9

Library of Congress Card Number 79-153403

Printed in the United States of America

All rights reserved

Acknowledgments

PULSE-Finger Press wishes to thank *The Beloit Poetry Journal* for permission to publish *The Kite,* and *Labris* for permission to publish *Lawn Mowing: Power Drive.*

Note: The title-page fingertip motif of PULSE-Finger Press *is a detail from the panel of the Sistine ceiling depicting the creation of Adam.*

PULSE-Finger Press
Box 16697
Phila., PA 19139

TO THE ONE THAT NEVER WAS

CONTENTS

Properly, we should read for power. Man reading should be man intensely alive. The book should be a ball of light in one's hands.

—*Ezra Pound*

BLOODLINES

The Kite

The sky was blind and blue and focused like
cataracts on Plato's cave, clamped
like stained-glass garbage lids on spectacles . . .
sighted on a sun that had slipped its string, a kite—
but steady since he could not see beyond
the glaring maw of the Minotaur—
a lozenge of light melting in the mouth of the labyrinth,
soaking the mazes with sunlight to relieve the sore,
the lockjaw against light that would make him see—
if not accept—the medicine of meaning in the phrase, "to
     be". . . .
It was a good day for flying kites—if
only I could escape my squalling son and willing
wife, slip the tugging mooring lines that tied
me to turf as placenta, plasma-colored beer as
amniotic brew. . . . "To be" intends to try; therefore . . .

Bloodlines

I grabbed the lumpy bobbin of string and fled—
as fast as my middle-aged legs could carry me across
the tufted field—fled the rising wail
standing skyward out of his widened mouth like
a stretch of string hypnotized by a fakir with a flute:
    that mouth was mere mirage, I knew, but the wail,
ah, the wail and the flared face and brat brain
were real, and I fled the bristling blond head and
blue eyes blurting anger and greed—loping,
I fled and the kite jerked from her hand and leaped
like a goosed gazelle, like a buckshot bronc, staggered
at the peak of its crazy climb, tugged frantically for
string—and plummeted to earth in a paper-crackling crash.
Panting, trying to laugh and call it fun, I stopped
and stared back at the sorry sight. My lungs burned,
my cheeks tingled, my knees trembled from the frantic
pressure my hyped-up heart was making to
keep pace with the needed blood supply:
                        the sorry
fact was, my heart had forgotten how to fly.
(What Plato called exile from the Empyrean, now
we call cholesterol.) A sorry sight, indeed,
I saw, when my head stopped spinning:
                      shattered—
spent as a piece of flak, as a spot of sperm
which had missed its target—the kite lay
as slack as my sleepless sex, its crumpled rag
tail curled like a sapless snake. From far
away, I could see—I could feel!—the kite twitch,
for the tremors raced along the string like an electric spark:
    a sudden gust of wind scooping the ground caught
and lifted, flipped it like a flapjack, and, for a second
as it skittered across the skillet, I thought it would take
off and fly—skim like a skeet, escape
like a flying saucer into the Martian mirages of
longing which haunt the human mind. . . . But the wind
died and the frying fish flopped

back into the pan, the kite sank
down to French fry in its own fat, cook
over the nuclear fires cooling at the earth's
core:
      it settled like an ear listening to a heart beat,
for the cooling earth is sclerotic to its soft
center—or will be when that molten clot is dry.
(The planet is a cherry-filled lump of chocolate,
a bonbon filled with pus like a boil. The galaxy
is a candy box God gave himself to keep from being
bored:
      Narcissus nibbles his own necessity.)
What happens when rock cannot pump out
through volcanic veins, fertilizing earth
with Krakatoa fires?
        ' There wasn't time to think:
  anxious to help, she was racing to the stricken kite,
hoping to hold it aloft at the tail-end, encouraging
a cleaner launch, giving the headstart needed
to get it off the ground. But he was racing
her to the kite—so much fury would shred the flimsy
shield caught in a tug of war—and it looked
like he would win:
        chunky legs churning, three-year-old
rage pumping adrenalin through smooth-bore
veins, his arms flailing in fury and his fisted
face scratching me with screams, pleading for a chance
to fly. I panicked and I fled. Again—confronted
with the face of fury, the fearless thrust to fly—
I fled. As he reached to grab the graceless form
of strings and sticks—for a kite is a solid sieve
until fleshed out, inflated with fat wind—
I jerked the cord in my hand with all my might
and ran, fled before she—a few steps behind
him—surely would have ripped the kite from
his fingers, tearing it from his infant confusion,
helpmate overtaking me with offers of help

I'd rather not have.
                 Jerked, the kite scraped
the ground, skittered beyond their clawing fingertips,
snagged on a hillock until the string was taut
enough to snap—and then sprang free, leaping like a marlin,
beautiful and fierce, shaking its head to cut
the tugging cord, wild falcon hooded
by world as a womb, unwilling to see the cord
as a tie to life, a buttonless umbilical grounding
the bird to the source of its lifeblood, earth:
                                 leaping,
the kite soared from the surface I was racing over
to keep my fish informed with flesh—reached
a peak again and staggered, tugging for string stronger
than I could pay it out—and dived to earth
again, its tail fluttering frantically, terror
making its tissue skin shiver at the prospect of plunging
back among the preying sharks, especially tethered
to my stick-axled reel. . . .
                    Frantic the kite
would crash, I raced across the storm-tufted turf,
hillocks booby-trapped with gopher holes, squalls
of grass camouflaging mosquito swarms, chiggers
and ticks churned up by my pounding feet. Squalls
of fire sear my esophagus, knots grip
my guts, my halfway-to-hell heart flutters
like a sail caught in a crossing wind, bangs
like a hatch loose in a head beleaguered by lashing
winds:
              my head is light and I am floating free
although I stumble and fall, feet snag in the surging,
wind-roughened surf. . . .
                  Gasping, light-headed from lack
of space and air, I race on nonetheless, determined
to make my sluggish kite soar, to fly despite
sagging muscles and a will weakened by too much
sleepy sex:

             bursting, I make one final
surge before turning back to see my kite
climbing vertically into the sun couched on my cupped
shoulder like a dazzling block of ice I am
delivering to hell:
             bursting—bribing myself
with the belief that I am Pheidippides bringing
the news of victory at Marathon—I make the final
assault and then turn back to see my kite
sink and soar—soar straight into the sun!
It's glorious! Coughing, spluttering to catch
my breath, chest heaving, I simply stand and pay
out line—not even that—more simply still,
just let the line slide through my fingers as I watch
the kite catch wind and sea-gull to the source, swoop
and soar like a hunting hawk released from its hood, sent
to slash liver from the sun. Sic 'em, boy!
Let slip the dogs of war! Unleash the hawk
to rip the liver from the rock-bound sun, prey
on heaven as mankind preyed on Prometheus!
Magnificent!, I cry, but inwardly, sweat pouring down
my face and sides, my swimming eyesight clearing
now, my heartbeat steadying as I watch the string
unspool in a clean smooth slide. . . . I wonder why
I feel tied to this kite like Prometheus to his rock,
the string in my fingers short-circuiting blood,
transfusing life from my liver into a stillborn ballet.
    The string burned through my fingers as it slipped away,
pulled by the climbing kite stabbing, slashing
upward to be free. . . . Once having pierced
a ceiling of dead air surrounding the earth, it seemed
the kite was free to soar, unhindered by dead
skin packed by atmospheric pressure into
callouses, membranes—earth's crust like a hymen
starving the stratosphere into sterility—
pierced by the kite like a surge of sperm, now watch
the spirochete wriggle to conceive the sun!

But
as I paid out line, my wife and son caught up
to me, she with her prideful hand on my shoulder,
congratulating my accomplishment, he
with his whine, shirttail-tugging demand to fly
the kite too—my turn, my turn!
Swiftly, the kite
had stretched out all the string, unreeled the whole spool,
and now was frolicking like a mutt on a mile-long leash,
still tugging to be free. What was there left
to do? I toyed with the notion of cutting the cord,
seeing if the fish I had hooked could live on its own,
swimming free in the stratosphere. Could it survive
without air to feed from, forage in to keep afloat?
But for a while I gripped the stick—wife and offspring
by my side—as if I were water-skiing
behind a powerful air-borne motor boat . . . and then
I imagined myself as Franklin waiting for
the storm to strike. . . . But the truth was that I
was breathing regularly now, the sweat was drying
on my skin and boredom had returned. The sun
was high and fierce, and even with a rising wind,
I knew that lightning could not strike. I shrugged.
What good would it do to cut the cord? The thought
seemed fanciful, at first—I tried to imagine the kite
caught up, swept into the holocaust at the center
of the sun, my kite—flimsy as a snowflake—transformed
into a cinder in the eye of God, perhaps even causing
a tear to hiss. . . . Squinting (I could barely see
it now), I spied the tailless diamond spread-eagled
against the sun—and shrugged, although the sharp
rays and sparkling surface stung and made
my eyes water:
wiping the tears away, I shrugged again—
although I watched a while, there was nothing to do but wind
it back. Cutting the cord would only make
the kite flutter, panic and plummet to earth far

out of sight . . . another Daedalus dead in a foreign
land. . . . And why should he be different from Icarus,
I thought, handing the naked stick to my pleading
son, tugging at my shirttails, stamping his feet,
frantic with frustration, fighting me for a chance
to fly? Why, indeed, I thought, passing him the stripped
stick, since one day I, like Daedalus,
would also die? . . .

             My wife's turn next to latch
onto the leash, walk the dog across the sky,
watch the capricious kite water lawns and trees
of the stratosphere, wagging its rag tail all
the while. And watching her reminded me of the myth
of Ariadne, the cunning lady who unwound the string
from the mouth of the labyrinth which made the Minotaur,
lining out the birth-trail which had to be retraced like
a white line down the center of the road. (Were U
turns allowed? Suppose the plumb line pointed one
way? How deep into the cave could Ariadne go?
Hobbled to his air hose, how deep can the diver plumb?
Watching her, I wondered how high the kite could get
through her guidance:

             how high can you get
on amniotic beer?) So watching her walk the dog
made clear why the cord could not be cut:
   each animal anchored the other, seesawing through time,
so the kite was fed by the stake it was tethered to,
mouth of the cave was connected to the anus open
and groping for bottom at the end of its rope. . . .
Standing there watching, a spasm of pride and fear
struck as my son—a blue-eyed blob with a face
unformed by the strains of flight—stuck his sticky
hand into mine and squeezed. Together, beside
the woman who had been the bridge, the conduit between us,
who had keyholed flesh down from the sun-riven sky
and shaped lightning strokes into a son with sticky
fingers and a candy craze, we stood and stared.

We shared neither comfort nor community.
Nostalgia and a sense of loss we shared, a sense
of sorrow because we could not regret
a sense of caring we could never know:
                                        love
is inherited like the color of hair, eyes and skin.
Thickening, paunchy, weighing to the grave with each
ingrained fungus-growth of fat, widening my grave
with each gravy-stain cell of girth added, I watched
a while longer—all three feigning interest in
watching the kite fly—and then we reeled her in,
and, dazzled from squinting at sunlight—without
seeing the sun—trudged home, blindly. Wound
around a dead stick, the ball of string felt
fat and sleek:
                    the stick was splinted, stuffed
by a taxidermy of wound spider webs. . . . In my other
hand, I gripped the kite at the cross-sticks
like an African shield:
                            the motto on the face was a tiger
rampant, tail coiled, eyes glittering and lips a-snarl.
The paper crackled and flapped on its skeleton of crossed
sticks like loose skin, the dewlaps of old
age, of kwashiorkor. From behind, the kite looked
as if someone had skinned its bones bare, the cross section
of dead flight crucified . . . trudging home a trio
of discontent. . . .
                        Delirious, at night he had
dreams, confused with the act of making love . . .
confused with contorted arms and legs, lips
sucking tight and tongues gripping like tentacles,
lashing legs and knotting knees, kisses
clotting like blood and dissolving in sighs, in spasms
of wonder and savagery, of doubt and delight, that
sperm and spit could flash the spark and leap
the space from *he* to *she,* from pole to spar,
transfuse the sweat of day into

the plasma siphoned, bled from sex—humankind's
remotest star:
                    drowning, splashing in
uncertainty and suffocating in the fight, confused,
he asked himself, *Is this my dream? Now*
am I dreaming of flying kites? Or did I fly
the kite today that I am dreaming of flying now?
Delirious, nonetheless he strained to pass
the lump clotted in his loins, he prayed to pass
the stone of gall he was rolling now like Sisyphus,
for sex was the struggle—oh sesame!—to reopen
seeds when the stone slipped away at the crest of the distant
roll, spasms shook the rock free:
                                    Am I dreaming now,
or was I merely awake this afternoon?
                                          Straining,
he struggled to keep the kite aloft, racing
as hard as his mattress-mired muscles would allow—
the bed pitching and rolling like a raft in a storm
livid with soaking lightning sheets—he worked
to roll the rock up the greased slope, straining
to keep his grip, with short stabs and long
lunges like an easy lope and keeping his eyes
fixed on the rising, storm-ridden kite the while:
Will it shred apart in this storm of sweat? Or
will the lightning flash and travel sooner, sped
on a conduit soaked in clouds, slashed by sun?
He lunged and saw the kite soar, leap for the sun
and disappear against the brutal glare, engulfed—
except for its flapping tail. . . . Against the glare,
he heaved and the kite leaped and the last of the string
suddenly slipped away and once again he was holding
a naked stick, anchoring a tugging kite
and finally convinced that he could not cut the cord:
for wouldn't the kite sag and simply fall away,
unsocketed, pulled from its roots like a watermelon plug,
unfed, raped to test the ripeness of the seeds

21

inside? He sagged with relief when the last of the string
spurted off the spool. For a while, he sailed the kite calmly,
relaxed, content to let the rock teeter on the brink
of coasting clouds—but toying with contentment, he soon
became bored. Tugging, diving and leaping, the kite
resisted, but he soon released his grip and the empty
stone rolled away, the string re-reeled as fast
as a rock clattering downhill. . . .
         Now he lay back,
drifting quietly, listening to her quiet breathing
fill the room with begging questions, large
and dark, questions they refused to ask because
they already knew the answers they feared to face,
felt were better smothered beneath the covers of bedding
and the equal dark of the quiet room, the smell
of sweat and sperm seeped into the sheets, rose
like smoke in the sunless space. *Am I dreaming now,
or was I earlier when I flew my kite? Or was I
kiting in sex, just now? Either way,
there is only so much string, I see, so much
weight the kite can carry in measuring its climb.* . . .
 Depleted, loathing myself for accepting
the emptiness of loveless sex—the cowardice
in convincing myself that pity was not a substitute
for experience—I sneaked out of bed (pretending
to be considerate, expecting silent congratulation
since I knew she was not asleep—in fact, was disturbed
by more than the prospect of my absence or creaking
mattress springs, crouched down into her own womb
of worry)—as stealthily as my trembling legs
would allow, I slipped from bed, and, dragging
on a dressing gown, forced myself—step by step—
through stages of depression as steep as walking in sleep,
rolling a rock up a hill of hate—I forced
myself into this room I call a den (a barren
bedroom with a shaky table where the bed had been),
a lair where I might lick my wounds and lie, write

this poem, I mean. *Lie or dream?* Force
myself—insist—that art is an affirmation of
the will to live, a record of man's past
power to recuperate from life's power to punish
him. I'm having trouble convincing myself,
however, that the old clichés can still make me care:
   maybe they lack force, for now I'm really being
forced to feel. . . . The trouble is that I do
believe:
           art is the healer—but only if
it is confrontation and not escape—truly
a mystic wonder and springs from the death-deep wish
to live, subconscious or otherwise—lodged
in Plato's sunlit state of dream. . . . But what
does it matter, if sex is simply a way of scratching
chigger or mosquito bites? Pulling off ticks
picked up by flying kites in an open field?
My son—the time-bombed lump from my loins set,
anchoring me to earth and ticking to explode in death—
and what of my legacy to him? The tock's
head bores into the blood and ticks off the stream,
deposits poison to whiten tissues out of blood
cells too rich to rot, creams pus boiling
to a head to burst, in time. Ripened, is the core
of my legacy a kite? Then what does it matter if the rickety
contraption I tried to ride on the lion winds of March cannot
weave pelvic lamb's wool of sunlight into
magic carpets loomed in any laps of time to soar?

An Avalanche of Now

Half awake, Quincy Slope struggled against sleep, but slipped back and drifted downhill in the dream. He shivered, rolled on his side and drunkenly smacked his lips reaching for the missing side of an expected kiss. It had always been there before, why not now? he wondered, but fell asleep again, smiling. He swallowed his side of the kiss dreamily. Drifting into sleep, he thought, I am not awake, I have merely been dreaming of myself awakening. Now I am no longer sleeping, I am dreaming of waking from a golden dream.

Now?

He tossed and was more awake. He lurched onto his back and realized he was trying to break out of dream. His breath grew steep. He flung out his arms and dimly sensed he was trying to simulate crucifixion. He smiled to himself and tried to unstick his eyes. But something held them, perhaps sensing he was really master of the situation and could waken if he chose. Sensing this, he smacked his lips and slipped back into languor. But this time he frowned. The habit of the dream kiss was gone, this time it hadn't felt even remotely there. Could the habit be broken as quickly as the dream?

The back of his neck was dull ache. The ache slid to the bottom of his spine like a keel slipping into water. He struggled to lift his head and panicked when he failed. The ropes of sleep still held. Apparently he hadn't quite been launched. He relaxed to await the baptism of the smashing bottle—maybe that would shake him up.

Now?

He was breathing heavily, his breaths grunts. His mouth was dry. He was forcing himself. His loins were dry, how many times had he already popped his cork and bubbled over—four? five?—and still he was lurching on, no pleasure in it, absolutely none, and yet he went lurching on, driven by some motive he couldn't identify. Was it fear? Shame? He could take as much punishment as she could, you'll see. He wouldn't be the first to quit—he couldn't! She couldn't say he wasn't all man, not Quincy, not smoothie Quincy Slope.

Was it fear? He grunted and relaxed. He sank into delicious sleep. But it irked him, somehow, that the pleasure he took in languor was lessened by a queer consciousness he couldn't quite black out. Try as he might, he couldn't black out the feeling that some part of himself was still awake, hovering above the bed like a black angel and smiling ironically. The feeling that some part of himself was alert and objectively regarding the other sleeping part annoyed him. He didn't like being laughed at, even by himself. It annoyed him that his other half wouldn't go back to sleep and enjoy the languor too. It was the detachment of the mocker that annoyed him. That was no way to enjoy yourself, standing apart and laughing at everyone. They won't like it, they want you drunken too. . . .

A damsel with a dulcimer
In a vision once I saw . . .
For he on honey-dew hath fed
And drunk the milk of Paradise. . . .

Secretly, he opened his eyes and peered around the room. Suddenly he was wide awake but pretended to be asleep. Someone was watching and he wanted to ambush the watcher, make him reveal himself—then *he* would pounce and sink fangs into the enemy.

Rather casually, he thought, he rolled his head from side to side. He would be cunning and surprise his foe.

Now?

He yawned, smacked his lips and stretched. He flipped back the sheet covering his naked body. He was getting set to spring.

The window at the foot of the bed was open. Dawn and a gentle breeze broke through the window together. A single ray of sunlight spilled over the windowsill and the wandlike shaft of light struck his bare foot and pricked it with a spark of heat. The warmth spread as if the spark had ignited a growing flame . . . drinking the milk of Paradise. . . . Dawn was breaking like a slow wet dream.

Quincy Slope, Quincy of the golden hair and creamy skin, lay back and caressed his body with a smile. Mentally he licked his body like a cat. He felt a soft surge of pleasure. He purred, spread his legs and stretched. The sunlit languor was delicious.

He was proud of his muscular legs, his flat stomach and narrow hips. He was proud of his greyhound sleekness, his deep chest and sun-tanned skin. He had put something over on mother nature, since everything had been a gift.

Now?

He peered out the window. He almost forgot his fear. There's something I must remember—but can't. He listened for the cats.

In the hazy distance, he could see the spire of Old St. Nick's. Like a moving mirage, the spire swam toward him until it was standing on the windowsill. He stared at the spire. It closed in and clarified like a specimen under a microscope. He wished he could believe in God, but Sarx Street was so real—how could you believe in anything down here? He longed for beauty, a beauty that would never die, but on the Sarx you saw too much. Maybe love, the right kind of love—a love that was more than just futile longing—was the answer he was looking for. But he had learned that you couldn't legislate for love. Either you had it and gave it, or didn't and you couldn't. Getting it was the problem, because that meant you had to give. How *could* others believe? That put him back where he began. Yet more and more lately, he felt a yearning, an increasing need to flow . . . outward. . . .

Now?

Through the haze, he suddenly heard the cats. They returned morning after morning to make love in the straggly garden beneath his open window. They were fond of the patches of dampness beneath the struggling flowers. He had tried to discourage them by throwing stones, but they always came back again. He learned to ignore them, finally. Damp and dirty, he shrugged, but to them it's paradise.

They burst into serenade. First singly, then the soloists joined forces and the yowls became a rooster chorus. Occasionally, a sideman cut out from the basic melody with a free-lance trill or two. But most of it was choral work. Their padded endless pacing had packed narrow paths beneath the skimpy shrubs. And vines cloaked fences like ragged clothes.

The shrieks peaked to a rooster pitch and stopped. Quincy listened for the yowling to begin again. He imagined the cats lifting their heads to howl, he could see them beneath the flowers and on the fences, singing and swaying to seduce a soulmate into kitten-soft copulation.

But she was there now, there on the windowsill, as fluid as a landslide and as light as his fingertips.

No, he groaned, no, not again. He closed his eyes and turned away. But the miniature mirage on the windowsill smiled: she knew he was watching out of the corner of his eye. She was a burlesque queen. Day was shedding night, but he couldn't shake the image, she appeared to him daily now. She was more and more necessary, was becoming a part of himself.

No, he groaned, no. He pushed his head into the pillow and rolled his face away. The ends of the pillow clamped his ears like bulging breasts.

No, no, no. But she knew he was inviting her yes, yes, yes, out of the corner of his eye.

The image stood on the steeple and the steeple stood on the windowsill. No, no, yes, no. Maybe if I keep very still, she will go away.

Now?

No! She was dangerous!

His hands were slick with sweat. He slid them down his thighs.

His hands leaped away. Then he laughed crazily. The steeple was in his lap. The steeple had leaped from the windowsill into his lap and she was still standing on its tip. He laughed again crazily.

He peeped down. It was still there, like the devil on the mountaintop. He opened his legs, hoping it would drop through the earthquake crack.

No!

Now?

The steeple was the spindle of a phonograph. Slowly, it began to turn. Slowly, she began turning too. He yowled like a mating cat.

She began to spin swiftly. She would become a whirling blur, a standing dust storm, a dainty tornado strong enough to rip him out by the roots.

He had to be cunning. He would sneak up behind and strangle her.

Catlike, his hands sprang and grabbed. He thought it

would sting like a porcupine. It was soft as a hard rubber hose. The fish on the line fought frantically.

He wrestled, but the fish was hooked and the battle for axle grease began.

No!

Now?

I got you! He threw back his head and howled. The breasts squeezed his ears.

The struggle was hard. The devil fish was cunning and wouldn't stop. The more he wrestled it away, the stronger it became, the harder it fought back.

I got you!

Now?

No!

The figurine was whirling like a wild weathervane. Her skirt spun out from her waist. Her thighs were naked. Her skirt rose higher as she spun. Her belly was naked too. She was on tiptoe. Her thighs were taught, her buttocks luscious, the body of a woman, moist and supple, a body made for love, sleek under a constraining dress but ample as mud, as grape pulp, when released. As she spun, her belly, thighs and buttocks swelled like a sponge soaking water, a mummy returning to life after having been embalmed. As the steeple and damsel spun, a rising whine, a single note of music swelled into an expanding wail. The vision grew like a dream expanding out of instant sleep, swelling beyond the shapes of skull, to engulf all of reality.

Yes!

No!

Now?

Spinning, her belly button winked like a lighthouse warning. Sandbars and shoals ahead! Her breasts, her buttocks, were sleek and ample as ceramic pottery. Smash them! See if the statue is full of milk and shit!

No!

Yes!

Now?

He groaned and thrust the thing away.

Then he cocked his head to listen. Under the rising wail, he sensed the distant tremor of an avalanche. The roar of self-love was growing, the rumble in the geyser's bowels was churning him up and down.

No!

Now?

He held his breath and pushed. He closed his eyes and wrenched his head away. His face was flushed. He could smell his own sweat. His stinging eyes blurred. It was hopeless and he knew it.

Yes!

He grabbed it with his left hand and pushed as hard as he could. He wanted to break it off. He wanted to rip it off so it wouldn't tempt him any more.

But he flung his right arm back and snatched the hankie from the table. He didn't have to look. His timing was perfect; practice makes perfect. In a sweeping movement he snapped it down and tented the hankie across the steeple. He would smother it.

He bandaged it in the hankie and grabbed with both hands. The hooked, bleeding fish fought back. The wail rose to a shrill peak and snapped off. The geyser erupted with a roar and stopped. The avalanche swept over him thunderously and subsided into a whisper of settling dust as it reached the bottom of the mountainside.

He smiled. He had caught the silken avalanche in his handkerchief. Nothing had escaped.

He went slack. He was deliciously exhausted but the fish had been landed. In its death throes on the deck, it quivered and lay still.

Now?

He looked into his lap. The pirouetting woman was gone. The mirage of steeple was gone. There it was, back in place on the windowsill.

The dawn was brighter now. Reality had solidified after dawn. The steeple was cold and clear on the windowsill. And below the sill, he reassured himself, was the golden dome of Old St. Nick's. He only had to stand to see where the steeple stood.

He looked into his lap. His flesh was a pink lollipop, a crimson blob on a soft stick, a succulent blur fading under the transparent, silken skin of the soaked handkerchief.

Though tired, Quincy mopped up the evidence carefully, being especially careful not to smear any of the filthy stuff on the nice clean sheets. He wiped his fingers like a surgeon before an operation. Then he squeezed the handkerchief into a sticky ball and dropped it between the bed and wall, the wall away from the bedroom door. He carefully wound himself in the sheet, sighed, smacked his lips and swiftly fell asleep.

No, there was no such thing as reality. Reality was a mere mirage. But isn't a mirage a reflection of a reality which *does* exist—somewhere?

Now?

Quincy's answer was a snore.

Wha-what?

Sentences

Sentences . . . full of high sentence? . . . I think
man is time serving a sentence . . . the same
sentence I serve my sex into
her showing slides . . . home safe movies of
staring through the shaved fish net of birth
at the boundaries of the sun king's system,
solar court satellites dancing like tennis
balls scoring points within the base lines of love, shooting
celluloid stars against the movie-screen sky, stag
leaps against chain link fences of gravity become
time servers staring at matinée stars, soap box
vacations in the spaces threaded by
visits projected between kisses of the equinox,
labial sprochets meshed among the astrolabes and light
in strobe, the zodiac of Ptolemaic spheres
sexualized by phrenology, phrenology equals

Bloodlines

phenobarbital when
sextant astrology is a branch I stared closely at
and saw that spring stars shooting from the roots of sex
were bloated with blood, nipple bullets
bulged and burned, quivered like sexes
sprocheting into spring, screwing themselves into
moist air, time lapsing into photo spaces, flesh
flashing in time between
the hair-strewn and the scudding stars. . . .

That night, my son, a bud himself, budding
sex still slung in a breechclout secured
with safety pins, marveled at the smear of stars
across the timeless sky: Daddy, look! Look
at all the stars! The streaming stars were a vapor
spoor dropped by an undiapered jet
strafing the riddled sky . . . fertilized
with words . . . machine-gunned into sentences . . . syllables
furrowed into sounds . . . seeds consonant with life and death
    into
caterpillars crawling—humping like omega,
flattening to make a dash for the beginning, loop
and dash and then begin again—the words are
sentences men serve spaced out in time
continual in the mind . . . as sections of
decapitated caterpillars crawling along a branch toward
avowals, the bulging bud
trying to finish the sentence before the end
of spring foils everything into a fetal sleep
spaced out along the same branch I was staring through
to see the smear of stars: Daddy, daddy! Look
at all the stars! The stars sparkled in the branches
I was staring through and made the bald, spidery
old elm seem a Christmas tree, the gray-bark branches
alive with sprints of light-bouncing buds that popped
open and spilled spores of sparks into
the sterile sky. Look, look at all the stars!

34

But I knew better. The bare branches—burning
with spring and blistering into buds—were much
closer than the distant stars, no matter how brilliantly
the stars did shine. Yet spring was closer, I told
myself, than tail light across eons, glimpses of past
glory reflected from a star that might be deader
than pupal light, an old elm blighted by winter's
loud bark. The Milky Way was monoxide waste
from a dead exhaust, sputterings from a sex long
since spent. I heard, Look at the stars! and saw
the words crawl across the branch spaced out
like a sentence across the sky and knew my brain
was the bud and cocoon the hairy worm was reaching for
and wondered: What happens when the blister at the bulge
of the branch breaks? Bud spurts into a blossom much
    better,
much closer than the stars? While its light wings
through space, the star may be cocooned in death;
sentenced from its source by distance, the programmed bug
also serves time in cycles to be a butterfly—
an awe-struck son, satellite of a sentence which
now spans space with light from a darkened source,
desolation which light years cannot serve. . . .

The
Carnival-Barking
Dolphin's Cry

Wha-what?

She shivered and tried to shut it from her mind. It's like a crazy dream! The old feelings coming back! As if the time between had never been. Oh, God! Some hungry evil was lunging out of hibernation in her heart.

Be careful, the boy is growing up. You can't keep the secret any more, a false step and your world will come apart. Damn you Stefan! After all these years! Hold on, she warned herself; you've been jumpy as a cat all week.

She raised her hands to dry her eyes and the rough money bag rubbed against her face. But remembering, her eyes went soft and bright with longing. Stefan! Her Old World lover reappearing after all these years! The wonder and the mystery of—

No! This is the New World. Let the boy be the tenderness you lost. But he's growing up, she sighed, some day he'll have to know his real father . . . the dark, secret side . . . the savagery of sex . . . the whole mystic side. . . . She shrugged and felt ashamed.

She went through the kitchen quickly and to her bedroom up the spiral stairs. She paused at the closed door of the boy's room half hoping to hear the sound of easy breathing. How sweetly she remembered him in sleep! She remembered the childhood times she had tucked him in, but all that was in the past. He wouldn't stand for it any more. She sighed.

A board creaked and roused her from her reverie. She went to her bedroom quickly, just across the hall. She had wanted to be near the sleeping child and the habit was too strong to break. He was the only thing she had, made all the suffering worth it, after all. But one day he would be gone. Well, that's the way it was. Loneliness, like love, was just a habit—the heartbeat, heartbreak, life itself was a habit too. He'll understand, some day, with children of his own. She sighed. But maybe it wasn't true. She hated her swarthy husband, in a way, but maybe that was just the point. Habits form when you can't open up your heart. Or maybe they are a way of hardening your heart. If only she had had someone else to love!

She pressed the money bag against her cheek and stroked it dreamily. But for Quincy, not some silly Pepsi-generation girl. What do they know? She hugged the leather bag between her breasts. To them, breasts are just a problem in how to fit a dress. A woman, a woman and a man, she said to herself and hugged the money bag. What do they know?

She roused herself and went to the small safe at the foot of her bed. The safe was camouflaged with an old, beautifully embroidered shawl. She had done it so long ago, hardly more than a girl, yes, the year we escaped to America. The design depicted an Old World hunting scene. A snarling pack of dogs baited a boar in a forest clearing. The boar was savage against the snapping dogs, slashing them with his bloody tusks. Soon he would escape the wounded dogs, but a mounted hunter charged out of the trees with an upraised spear. He was laughing and the plumes in his hat bobbed in the morning breeze. The nostrils of his charger flared. Golden curls ringed the band of the hunter's hat. The horse too seemed eager for the kill. Gay sidesaddle ladies ringing the clearing behind the merry hunter had their hands poised, ready to approve with polite applause. Pointed pines reared in the background, and beyond the pines, steeple-pointed mountains reared.

She threw back the shawl, worked the combination and deposited the money bag. The bag had the fluid heft and feel of a scrotum. She banged the thick, bantam-tough door and spun the knob. She tested the door and re-covered the safe with the embroidered shawl. She stood beside the safe and nodded at the hunter. He laughed back and poised his beribboned spear. She smiled. He had become a guardian spirit.

She looked around. The room was as bare as a clearing between the walls. It was dominated by a big double bed. Solid and covered with summer sheets, the bed pushed out from the wall like a granite slab of glacier, like a terrifically slow second growth, an underbrush of ice coming back to camouflage the scars of clearing. There was hardly room for weeds around the walls.

At the head of the bed, a faded copy of Botticelli's "Primavera" hung on the wall in a faded gilt frame. The picture had been cut from a magazine, pasted onto cardboard and covered with windowglass. How long ago had it been left in pawn?

A window at the foot of the bed faced onto the backyard and over the rooftops of Circle City. She could see the cross-topped steeple of Old St. Nick's in the hazy distance. The rooftops shimmered in sun. Waves of heat rose from the softened roofing tar. The gilt cross flashed. All looked like a faded dream.

The steeple and the spear. She shrugged and drew the green shade on the window and turned away. The glare had hurt her eyes. Sun flashing on the cross was sharp. She was grateful for the gloom. It should have been done this morning, but she had forgotten to draw the shade. It gets too hot for sleep.

There was a straight chair at the head of her bed on either side. A small closet for the Sunday best. A small chest at the bottom of the closet contained bed linen in pancake stacks. The room was stripped to essentials, like a woman giving birth.

She stroked the cool sheets on the heavy bed. Every morning she made it carefully, first thing. This she never forgot. In the warm green gloom, the white sheets glowed like altar cloths.

Their bedroom and *their* bed, she thought, and the thought was a little shock. She had never thought of it quite that way before. It had always seemed hers, and everything had been for Quincy. But the man had always been there— like the sheets and the shade and the steeple—and she realized she was glad. He was necessary now, especially when she was thinking of someone else. . . . Habits were so hard to break.

She remembered the first time they made love. Hardly more than a girl she was, but a woman, an old woman too, in far too many ways. He had promised to make her forget and almost did. With the work and worry and new baby, she *had* almost forgotten, had forgotten for days, for weeks, for months at a time—almost. It wasn't his fault the memory kept coming back, it wasn't his fault they couldn't create memories to drive the old ones out. . . . Maybe habit would.

Standing in the gloom, staring at the softly gleaming bed, she remembered his fierce little eyes, she remembered wanting to lie down and his grunting no. He thought she was trying to resist, but she was willing, she had accepted him for what he was, agreed to the arrangement—for the sake of the child, she reassured herself—but she didn't know what to do. What did he expect? But she was willing. He was no beauty, he was a man, but did he have to be so rough? She shivered and reassured herself: it was necessary for the child. She had something to be grateful for.

He pulled her from the bed and forced her up face-to-face. In the moonlight streaming through the window, his body shimmered with sweat. His black wiry hair glistened in the moonlight. She was fascinated, he had never been like this before, always so mild and kind. The baby was out of her body, and now he acted as if he owned her. She couldn't decide whether she liked it that way or not. His sweat made her nostrils twitch and burn.

Shattered specks of moonlight, scattering drops of mercury, glittered in his eyes. Sweat swelled at his temple and trickled down his cheek. Tufts of black hair bristled on his shoulders. His arms were slick with sweat. Fierce and dark and wordless, he was silhouetted against the moonlit window . . . swirling towards her now. . . . Through the open window, she could see the moon was full. Looming in the window, he eclipsed the silver coin balanced on the spire.

No!

She shrank and crouched back on the bed. She was willing, please . . . but she could take it better lying down. . . . The shadow in the window was hard and black and outlined in silver light.

No!

But her bare legs bumped the cold sheets and made her shiver. She was trapped, the dogs were at her heels, he was closing for the kill. There was nothing left but to turn and fight. She wanted to bay the moon.

"Yes," he said. Knots of muscle under his ears twitched in the moonlight. Only the baby was in the house, but the man had locked the door. Could he shut out her memories?

He stripped without a word. He stripped her fiercely, ripping her chemise. She was taller by a head, even in her naked feet. Their clothing tangled on the floor and drifted seaward in the moonlight.

41

Stunned, she was numb against his naked savagery. What right did she have to shame?

She would show him. He's like all the rest, she thought.

But she shrank away. His hard-on hairiness was disgusting. There was no sunlight glinting in *his* golden hair. She hated him with all her heart, but she was trapped. She was an instrument of his pleasure, nothing more. So she would use him too. That was better than indifference. You love it, he said over and over again, hissing into her ear. No, no, yes!

He grabbed her around the waist and pulled her in. His sweaty arms squeaked against her flesh as he strained her tight. Her arms hung over his shoulders and down his hairy back. She was sickened by contact with his hairy chest, the slippery hair along his back. She almost lost her balance and would have fallen when he grabbed, but she grabbed his head and buried it between her breasts and gripped his back with her fingernails. Seeds of blood seeped out of his sweaty skin. The stinging sweat was an antiseptic. Blood and sweat began to trickle down his back. He groaned and rubbed against her belly.

His stiff penis bent against her belly and she winced away but he gripped her waist and pulled her in. She grabbed his head, sucked in her belly and pushed her buttocks back and tried to shrink away. But the pointer's tail pursued, quivered like a compass needle aiming at its northern quarry. The tip of his penis tapped and flickered against her flesh like the antenna of a blind night bug seeking light. He pushed, stabbing with his hips, blindly aiming for the soft place where it would hook and hold, and, in sinking, seal the gap. He wanted to romp the burning coals, char his wings against the burning glass. He whimpered like a child for a lost toy, candy in a windowcase, mamma, mamma, I need the bathroom now, now, wailed the child. She closed her eyes, grabbed his ears and pressed her face into the glistening hair on the bullet head.

Stop, stop, she couldn't stand it, she was terrified, it was enormous but she pressed against it, twisted in his arms and pressed against it with her hip trying to squash the bug, but she couldn't bend it, the itch wouldn't go away, relentlessly scratched back. Stop it, I can't stand it any more, and roughly he twisted her around again, stop that or I'll break your goddamned back, you dirty rotten whore! The crawling bug began to tickle and she almost laughed.

Calmly, in a lucid moment blocked out of the terror, she lifted her leg and stepped over the feeler and pressed her hips into his. The gap was closed. Let the bug burn to death on the outside, crawling over the hot surface of the globe. He fought, but she grappled with all her might, trapped his arms under her sweating armpits and wrestled him quiet. If he cracked the glass, the vacuum would be broken and the light would go out. She was afraid of darkness—no! Blind bugs need the burning bulb to zero in.

She sniffed his skin. The room was filled with the smell of grilled flesh, the smoky stench of a sweat-greased barbecue. Flaming drops of grease, sparks of sweat dripped from his singed skin. Running fires flickered along the floor and smoky flames licked up the walls. Mixed smoke and moonlight drifted across the room. The silver-grey haze stung her eyes.

She locked her legs around the thing so he couldn't stab his hips. But then it became slippery with sweat and began to slide. She gripped her legs tighter but it was no use. She couldn't hold it. Frantically she realized she was fighting against herself. She was leaking grease. The trombone began to slide. She heard the music of mating cats.

He growled. He squirmed his sweaty fingers free. He pinched her armpits and she gasped and the handcuffs sprang open.

She felt his slippery hands sweep down her back. His fingers found the tight line between her buttocks and began to pry the hams apart. She hardened her haunches against his hands but the fingers pried until they had found the place.

He chuckled to himself. He pried lower and squeezed

with all his might. He read her like an open book, who was she trying to kid, but she was a little stiff from lack of use, if she fought the spine would crack. You love it, you love it socked in hard and deep. No, no, yes! He slipped her the word.

Suddenly she went slack. Her knees became rubber, her hams became fluid slush. Her skin began to slip. He sucked her breasts: the meat was done. The taste was milk and sweat.

He pulled the hams apart until she winced and thought the place would tear. Slumped on his shoulders, she could hardly stand. She opened up. The cats began to croon.

He slung back his rubber hips and drove in, once, twice, and then, pulling back his hips and poising like a slingshot, he let the rock fly and drove inward and up and he was there, glued to magnetic north. As slippery as butterbasted liver. Oh stop, I can't stand it any more! When would it ever stop? But with a yelp, he pushed harder against the place and felt himself sinking through the quicksand until he was afraid. Suppose he fell through to the other side of the reeling world? He'd dogear a page or leave a bookmark to blaze the trail. He gritted his teeth, took a firmer grip and pushed ahead. He stretched on tiptoe, gave one last tug and their hips were locked. Lost in the dark wood, Hansel and Gretel had sprinkled crumbs.

Suddenly she went slack. Her knees became rubber, her gaff was in the gill. The fish would fight, but it was firmly hooked. She threw back her head and bayed the moon. He buried his face between her breasts and began to stab with his bony hips. With his legs spread between hers, he bulled them both up and down, up and down, his heels bumping on the floor. The fires flickered at his heels. He was dancing on the coals. The cats began to shriek. The pointing dog flushed the quail and the world was filled with the wild whir of wings as they rose against the flaming moon. The hunter threw up his gun and fired. There was a loud pop as the bug banging against the hot glass broke the bulb. The cats became quiet and everything went black.

She closed her eyes and tried to wince from the stabbing pain, but his arms locked her waist and strained until she thought her spine would snap. No more! He was scribbling on the pages with shortening strokes in a drunken script. No more! But she began pushing against the pain. A spasm of delight made her laugh despite disgust. The ripping passed until there was only pleasure and a tight serenity. The rock before the tomb was rolled away. He slipped the bookmark in to mark the place for future reference. He wanted to remember where she rose from the dead and came back to life.

Deep below the billows, she heard the boar snort, the dolphins bark and the swift deadly swish of the closing sharks, but she rode the billows, and on the surging surface, spray, wind and the warm roll of heaving current seemed to wash her clean. As she threw back her head and closed her eyes and her hair tugged at her temples as it streamed backward in the wind, she caught a glimpse of the merry hunter plunging towards her on horseback with his spear poised to strike. Out of the billows he rose, the plumes of his hat floating on the wind like streaming spray and the hooves of his white charger thrashing the sea to foam as the charger reared and plunged and the rising sea plunged and rolled. Then the charger's mane, the plumes of the hunter's hat and his poised spear, all dissolved in flying spray. They shuddered and toppled to the bed.

He sprawled on his stomach and gasped, his arms helplessly by his sides. She shrank away and carefully wiped herself with the sheets. It was no use, the spray was too deeply flung. Conceiving was like having faith in God. It could happen against your will. You had to plan against it; abortion was artificial and too late to get the root. It always left a scar. Block it with your mind! Blind faith was like being raped. Nobody can force your love, she thought. They can't make you love the monster of your lust. The man began to snore.

45

For a long time she was afraid to sleep. She lay on her back listening to the dying tremors of the avalanche. Her body twitched and ticked like cooling steel. Moonbeams and dust motes settled to the floor. Smoke and the smell of burnt flesh became faint and disappeared. The bed was cold and white and seemed to drift at anchor in the moonbeams. She strained to hear the cradled baby in the next room cry: it was past his feeding time. Thank God, he had slept the night through: her breasts felt dry.

Wide-eyed with fear, she crept closer to the sleeping man. She covered his shoulders with her arm. The sheet was streaked with blood as if dozens of bedbugs had been rubbed out by hand. Blood dried under her fingernails.

She lifted her leg, gleaming in the moonlight, across his naked hips and held him until, weary with wide-eyed watching, tired of listening for the baby's cry, her head sank on his shoulder and she also fell asleep. The moon waned and the first light of dawn shimmered on the windowsill. An animal, but at least he was alive.

She woke with a start in the cold, clear light of dawn. He was clamoring into her lap. He rolled her over and opened her thighs with a thrusting knee. He didn't have to waste time, she was hooked on the stuff, whether she believed or not.

She hugged him and closed her eyes. It didn't hurt so much this time. But the top of his head butted under her chin. There was no sound or smell.

She turned her face away. She tried to lift her head to kiss him. He thought she was still resisting and pinned her shoulders with his elbows. He'd break her yet, goddammit, he'd break her goddamn back. What's the use? Let him have his way—how can I ever win?

She longed for a face to face kiss, a mouth to muffle her whimpering. This happened once before! It's like a recurring dream! She tried to remember her beloved's face, imagine *him* here, weighing on her breast. She strained her face to kiss. Stefan! But when she opened her eyes, the face above hers in the darkness was framed in a bright black beard, was snearing and had glowing eyes. She remembered! No! She closed her eyes to shut it out. She tugged at his shoulders to pull him above her breasts, breasts she had proudly offered to Stefan, but he was hooked under down below and could not come, would *not* be humanized with a kiss. Stefan! Like doubting Thomas, men have to stick their fingers in the holes, and even then they don't believe. Love? The baby began to cry.

She bit the pillow and he was pleased to have provoked her passion: it was a tribute to his prowess. But it was dirty of her to squeal in sex. He thought she was a pig.

He finished and fell asleep. She got up and crossed the hall into the baby's room. He was red from screaming and continued screaming until she pushed her nipple into his mouth. Fresh light through the window shone in the golden down on the baby's head. She rocked and crooned, but he chewed her nipple with soft gums for a long time before he fell asleep. She kissed the flushed face, tucked him back into the cradle and went back to bed. The sheets were soggy with sweat, but she felt pounded to a pulp and swiftly fell asleep. Black sunlight shimmered in her hair.

A short time later, a bum pawned the "Primavera" above her bed. When it was not redeemed, she hung it on her bedroom wall. Her hard dark husband never noticed. Perhaps he might have shrugged. You have to make allowances.

"Maybe I haven't made much of a wife," she said and looked aroung the room. But he never seemed to care as long as he was satisfied. And everything was peaceful, had been hidden into place. The boy had been her peace. The years had made her bitter, but anyway, she had survived. And now? Had it been worth it? Was now worth fighting for— and how much? She smoothed the sheets lovingly and quickly left the room.

She crossed to the boy's room to make his bed. Otherwise, everything was neat and clean. And yet his nightmares were bad and getting worse. Almost every morning now his whimpers and cries reached her across the hall. She had begun waking automatically to listen for the cries. Careful not to wake the man, she slipped out of bed at dawn to listen behind his door. How many nights had she spent lying awake listening? She had thought he would outgrow the dreams, but she was afraid to invade his room any more: he would hate her. Now he was starting to remember the nightmares after he awoke. After a final glance, she quickly left the room.

In the kitchen, she locked the door into the pawn shop and washed her face at the built-in sink. Then she held a wet rag across her eyes. She wrung out the rag, hung it on a hook near the sink and fixed herself some food.

She made a stack of thick ham sandwiches with pumpernickel bread. She covered the sandwiches with a napkin. She sat, lifted the napkin as if to sweep dirt under the rug, and dug one of the sandwiches out. The thick slice of ham between the lips of the black bread reminded her of a woman's sex. No—the stacked sandwiches were folded handkerchiefs. But she remembered a cow from a farm in the old country. They had been watching her for weeks, waiting for her to drop a calf. She was excited. She had wanted to see what birth was like. But the cow was too sly. One day she was gone and it took them an hour of frantic searching in the high grass of the lower pasture before they found her once again. She had already dropped the calf.

She reached them first, but the cow was already on her feet and licking the wet calf and trying to make it stand. She nudged it with her dripping nose. Elastic streamers like human snot hung from the cow's nose.

The cow turned to place herself between the calf and the staring girl. She saw the cow's bony hind quarters. Something like a dirty rag was dragging on the ground. It was attached somewhere under the cow's tail by what looked like a long intestine. The intestine was purple and bloody. It broke under the cow's tail from the weight of the dirty rag. The rag was lavender in the sun. Smoke rose from the rag, and flies swarmed in the smoke.

The cow stopped licking the calf, turned and lowered her head to watch the girl. After a while, reassured that she was harmless, the cow began to eat the intestine and dirty rag. No wonder she had wanted to be alone.

While the cow was eating patiently, pausing to look at the girl from time to time, the calf struggled to its feet and wobbled to the cow. She turned sidewise to the calf. The calf didn't know what to do.

Then the farmer ran up, looked at the tableau and laughed. He was relieved that she was all right and the calf had gotten to its feet. If they don't rise a certain time after birth, they sicken and die, he said.

He went to the cow and tried to pat her head. She lowered her head and shyly hooked her horns at him. But he talked softly and she let him reassure her. He patted her head and whispered to her lovingly. Then he took a big red handkerchief with white polka dots out of his back pocket and wiped her nose. He treated her like a lady. He wiped his hands and brow on the handkerchief and stuffed it back into the pocket of his jumper. The cow knew she had done well, that the farmer was very pleased. She sensed that she deserved his care and let him have his way.

After stroking her head and telling her how proud he was, he gently pushed the cow around. He went over to the calf. The baby was frightened and shied away. As the farmer approached, it tried to run, but its legs buckled and it collapsed to its knees. It struggled but could not rise.

The farmer went to his knees, embraced the baby's head and spoke to it lovingly. There was terror in the baby's eyes, but then it realized that he meant no harm. He called the calf baby, his little lamb, and said what a fine calf he was and what a fine bull he would become.

Then he rose and picked the calf up, lifting it under the chest and tail. The cow was watching him closely, her head lowered at the farmer. But he carried her baby to the cow, stood the calf on his feet and forced his nose against her heavy udders. The baby didn't know what to do.

He stooped, grabbed one of her teats and squirted milk into the baby's face. The calf was blinded and sneezed and backed away. He licked his nose. He tasted milk and stood there, weaving on his fet, wondering. Then he wobbled to the cow and poked his face at the cluster of teats. But he didn't know what to do.

He grabbed a teat, held the baby's head, twisted up the teat and forced it between his lips. The calf began to suck.

The cow swung her head around to see what was going on. When she saw the baby sucking and the farmer watching with a smile, she turned away and began munching the rag again.

The farmer's wife, a heavy woman with a red face and a double chin and a polka dot handkerchief around her head, lumbered up. She was excited and hollered and flapped her fat arms. The cow shied and the calf lost its teat.

The farmer shouted for his wife to shut up, steadied the cow and gave the baby back his breast. Then he went to his wife. She waited with her head lowered and her rough, fat hands clasped across her rounded stomach. She looked as penitent as a peasant in the village church, but the farmer didn't care. She had borne many children, she should know better than all that noise. He paused and then smacked her across the mouth. She saw the wife's big breasts bounce with the shock of the sudden slap. He grabbed his wife by the elbow, spun her and pushed her away. "You're too late. Go back to the hay and pigs," he said. Without a word, she went.

He turned back to his cow and calf. His armpits were soaked with sweat. He was a big ruddy man with a blond stubble on his chin and cheeks. The front of his pants was wet with milk. He tugged off his straw hat and wiped his face on his sleeve. "A fine cow, a fine cow and calf," he said. "A good bull. Much money at the market." Then he replaced his hat and beamed. In the glaring sun, his eyes were deep in green shadows under the brim of the faded straw.

The cow lifted her head and mooed. It was a low-pitched lament. She swung her flank away from the calf and her teat plucked from his mouth with a little plop.

She lumbered to the farmer and began to bellow. The calf tried to follow but his legs were too shaky. He dropped to his knees and rolled onto his side. With his head lifted, he watched the cow. The baby's wet side heaved. Wisps of smoke curled out of his drying skin. His black hair shimmered with a purple sheen. The farmer laughed as the cow butted his chest with her wet nose. He slapped her neck, grabbed her horns and pushed her around.

"I know what she wants," he said. "The little fellow wasn't taking it out fast enough. Her bag's too full. It's heavy and the strain hurts," he turned back and explained to the little girl. "Some day, my little lamb, you'll find out too," he said. Then he squatted in the deep grass and began to milk her out. The girl watched the deepening puddle grow green in the sweet grass between his knees.

"There won't be enough for baby," she said.

"Oh yes," he said. "I want to relieve her a little bit." Nervous and shy, the girl watched.

"It's a shame to waste it," she said. The farmer laughed and shook his head.

"Yes. I should have brought a bucket. We could feed it to the pigs. But it would hurt to walk her all the way back. It's worse than waste to make her wait. But she's a good old girl, there's plenty where that came from," he said and slapped her side. She turned back to look at the farmer and began to munch her cud.

The little girl turned away. She followed the farmer's wife for a little while and then, very careful not to soil her frock, she leaned forward and vomited into the grass. Her vomit didn't look anything like the milk, but slowly it turned green too.

Her boots and shins were splashed. She stooped to wipe

them with her bare hands and then wiped her hands on her
frock. Then she lay on her back and for a long time stared
at the vast blue sky. The vomit smelled sour. But for a long
time she played a game with herself, wondering what animal
shapes the fleecy clouds assumed as they drifted across the
sky. The height made her feel afraid. She clutched the long
grass by her sides, braiding her fingers into the hair. She
felt she might fall off the earth, endlessly fall forward into
the big and empty sky. Finally she fell asleep in the blazing
sun to the sound of hunting bees and a boil of flies buzzing
above her vomit. She slept with her hands pressed against
her belly. She needed a home, her papa said, so he hired her
out to the farmers in the region while he peddled throughout
the countryside.

When she woke, her fingers were stained with grass.

Wha-what?

She sat up with a start. The farmer was kicking the
bottom of her boots. She jumped up. He grabbed her arm,
grabbed the back of her neck, bent her over and blistered her
with a switch for dawdling along the way. He switched her
for the grass stains on her frock. He had cut the switch to
drive the cow. Yoking the calf across his shoulders, he drove
them home with the whistling switch. Wha-what?

The puddle of vomit had dried when she sneaked away
from her chores and went back the next day, but the sour
smell was in her nose. "There, there," the farmer had said,
"don't cry. What's a few stripes, it means I love you? Next
time, don't stain your back."

Wha-what?

Miss
Laid Raggedy Anne
Spills Stuffing Through

miss
laid raggedy anne spills stuffing through
the lair between her lumpy legs
her hard
bitten
crotch clamps across the long lunar probe
of sterile strategies computerized to score
before the russians do
rocket to the moonside of silence to
nowhere
claim stakes through the vampire's heart of
nothing
driving flagpoles through the coffin lids where legionnaires
are vacuum packed in their craniums till dawn
perks their bloodlined claims to nothing up
coffee instant claims to vacant craters and cold

Bloodlines

war promontories of artificial lust tear
surfaces
skin so now
the stuffing bulges
out like blossoms of pubic hair
a casket-lining comforter of menstrual osmosis
against
his male prehensile sex between
where the vampire penis lives till dawn
and slips from the casket into limp sleep
coiled upon
sargasso she
dripping chinese water torture seeds upon
birth
bursting through the cotton bones
the low-ball bones built upon boll-weevil marrow
hard
bitten silk worm seeds
down
pupating like blackbirds baking in a pie until
metamorphosed
vampire cocoon in a long night of coffin cries
   savage I was savage
   tearing at raggedy's annie and she ripping my back to beds
   clinging with bat claws up
   side down like a swinging belle bow
   legged under wraps around my harrowing hips
   in hell to clapper clang clang clang salvation
   slung went the trolley car up the funicular slopes
   of picturesque San Francisco as
   her shrieks and my shreds stung in long lopes
   towards the sunbursting distant hill
   top
   ped
   alling down my shanks her stuffing fell apart
   while I was climbing the ski slope to zoom
   down the ski jump into soaring

54

far-flung flight without Icarian wings
to melt me down to splash
down down down
into sea mold around me in candle-dripping death
as my arms baled her in
and out she fell in death
my boating arm-loops locked together like barrel staves
her in on a baled
out stuffing came apart without a parachute
and down we both fell into unharrowed hell
down down down
brainpanned into the hammocks of
brass-intentioned bras
doublebarreled cells
padded like foam rubber cobblestoned
into a dilemma of death so surreal in clarity
I was wide-eyed in her dream
when raggedy anne died
I plucked aimlessly at the dirty stuffing
leaking through her missile-cracked crotch
birth-barked canoe
as david slingshot the moon through her arbalest legs
and goliath laid on her rapids back dead
aimed
button eyes nailed to her head with thread
cross-haired through holes in the center of her sights
telescopic x's cancelling the needle-pointed
compass-aimed setting of paradise
on a flesh-bound spaceship doomed to rescue nothing
more and more
than sterile
   tinker toy sex is political pocketball
cold
   missile-mongering is boy scout
war
   merit badges on the
rocks

Lawn Mowing:
Power Drive

Shamed by what the neighbors might think,
or power-driven by the compulsive need
to keep concupiscence neatly curbed, trimmed
like the balding hairline of a lawn cut back
from the concrete boundaries of a drive and overdrive,
clutch and floor-gear grabbing into gardens to keep
them flower-boxed:
                either way, the fight against
weeds is wieldy and by the weak, made so by summer
heat and lightning storms, blood-warm and wild
with only weapons made by man to barber thunder
back:
        everywhere I look—in winter, lurking
in ambush beneath the snow, microscopic madness
crystallized into a catatonic trance, poised

upon the brink of thaw and crouched to spring in heat
without a creak, savage seeds into the sun, spurt spores
into the sky like blood jerking from a jagged jugular—
in summer, blood cells spray into the air like streams
of seeds, soap bubbles streaming from the snow-cone heads
of dandelions, blown comettails bursting out of scrotum-like
symmetry:
        everywhere I senses am, for protoplasm smears
my sight and stuns my smell and rings my sound
with decibels of dancing bells, grand balls
banging in their pelvic belfries, belle-clappered cocks
swinging upside down like sleeping bats,
each thunderclap proclaiming liberty cracks throughout
the syphilitic land:
        a rover, wherever I power
drive my four-wheeled lust, I smellsound the same
pollution from the Pauline epistle proclaimed
in flaming touring tongues and revered as a highballed foot-
    light
opening a one-night grand stand in the company crotch
of the Old true North Church; the Apostle of the Gentiles—
that cowbird halfbreed, mixing his drinks—thus nurtures
nits in the nest of WASPs, prompting opening
midnight in the North:
        Scarlett, honey, now it's "A" fever
curtains time! For the Seventh Cavalry Yiddish are coming,
the Yiddish are coming! And if the weapons wielded
against weeds can sprout like sabres giving suck, divining
rods sucking springs out of desert hillsides, rifled mini
balls sprout sterile lead seeds that blossom into blood,
and powder horns of plenty convert into flintcocked
cornucopias, why should not the winter-starved weeds
awakening in pioneer kibbutzim everywhere?
My wife answered by nagging me to mow the lawn.
My son answered by flaring into a fit, tantruming
as badly as a baby losing its nursing tit.
I wunna help, too! I wunna help, too! In the end,

his curiosity overcame the snarl of my boredom, my rage
to get it over and done as quickly as possible:
   coitus interruptus is bad enough, without
complicating it further by running interference
like a nose that needs a good hard blowing to keep
it free and clear. Besides, I figured—betraying
as I thought it, the fruit of my learning and instinct as
a social wolf—it might be fun to play
father in the Hollywood way, for once
                             (which is
not always in the family way)
                        developing
celluloid frames of compassion and reference, humors
and honor, wisdom and grace, sped on a sprocket
and grease painted on a distant screen by dint
of a footlighted fantasy:
                    I sighed and figured to run
it through for one Virginia reel:
                       if it worked,
I could have it programmed for a Mack Senate playback:
                                   if

rôle-calling couldn't revive the transplant, I shrugged,
well, shit, just let the belle bomb on the cutting room floor.
No use hoping to gross and curtain call anything
out of a cellulose cold turkey carpetbagger like
Lazarus. Little did I know; but, gravely, began.
First, I said, mentally donning my jodhpurs and
D. W. Griffith Birth-of-a-Nation stance
and megaphone, ascot and cube-K sheet, first,
I said, son, you have to clear the way for
the cash to Carrie later crying in the wilderness:
                                 make

straight rum the way of the bored! And so,
holding his demon-honed hand, I shepherded him
around the yard, a bird, a lambsized lump
of blond lard glistening in the sun and cooing
with contentment because he was helping Daddy. So, first,

Bloodlines

I said, you have to police the area,
arresting all passion and throwing the hot rocks n roles
in jail. Which we did, scouting the jungle surfaces,
raking up sleeping sicknesses, collaring
the limestone dog dung, dodging the gopher holes
and booby traps of mosquitoes bursting
from ambush with every unwary step. The open
sun was a sneaking spy, sapping strength, seeping
into bones to X-ray secrets of life out of marrow,
freeze-fry man's mortality a dead infrared:
  soon my skin was smeared with the sweat of espionage
and the child was panting, by dint of my example, for
we had ripped out a few secrets of our own:
  rocks, empty beer and soda bottles; dead branches
and broken toys; abandoned dog bones and bits
of holy bread:
              soon the loaves and fishes were basketed
and the fragments piled into a heap on the concrete driveway,
awaiting conversion into a sacrificial fire, leaping
tongues levitating some miraculous monk's skirts,
rising on the tithes of Savonarola's grub stake,
hoping the Puritan prospects of gold deadpanned
out. . . .
          At first—perhaps foreseeing the need,
nay, even the necessity, of boredom—I had
sought out the different ways to mow the lawn and know
the word each time I had to go:
                              starting first
at this end and then the other, swathing designs
in the grass I cut, tracing tics out of tac toes
into the total tapestry, I tried everything to keep
the passion in the subplot of pubic grass
to be shorn, spurting protoplasmic earth more
than passionate floorplay, a game of replenishment:
  but even new toys—a new power-drive mower,
for example—couldn't keep the game alive. In fact,
the power-drive mower reenforced what had already

become mere rote. Game it never should
have been, that was the fatal flaw; yet game
it had to be, given the rules allowed
by law and necessity. Law became a habit
and love became routine. Even planting new
flower beds soon became a bore. Lucky
I was that someone who had been there before had
foreseen my need and invented this marvelous
machine, an automatic mower with front-wheel drive:
   throw in the clutch, and the front wheels grip
and pull; all you have to do is ride. Pushing down
the handle—using the rear wheels as pivots—raises
the rolling front wheels free of the ground and reminds
me of a giant bug on its back struggling
to twist upright; of a rearing horse hacking
the air with his hard front hooves; of the giant of Greek
mythology, Anteus, who lost his strength when his life
left the ground—
               but dropping the wheels down
bites them into the earth's back and pulls
you behind an unchained dog on a leash. The mower
reminds me of my sex, I sighed; all you have
to do is sit and steer, and, like pedigrees
of boardom, they have Toros now with the strength of a pig
so you can get the job done with even less work.
How did they manage in the days before power drives?
Can you imagine going back to hand scythes and sickles?
To wrestling roots from the earth with your bare hands?
To eating meat raw?

           I shrugged idle
speculation off and lapsed into my rutting
routine:
             even with my "helping" son trotting
alongside, hanging onto the handle like a stirrup,
I was done in no time at all—once I had cleared
my mind of all conceptions:

Bloodlines

                       I put the lawn
to bed in an empty dream:
                         soon the lawn was rolled
and trimmed, robbed of its tweedy currency and shorn
as tight as a dressed bedsheet, was as wet with sex
and meaningful as freshly minted newspaper sheets.
Yet I read the long lawns—following the wet
wheel-and-swath lines with a mental fingertip—
and was vaguely dissatisfied, like an illiterate lost
in a labyrinthine lavatory, unable to decipher the museum
signs of The New York Times:
                      Men or Women? Sink or Split?
A shiny renaissance of Playtex plastic tits
replaces Boticelli's Venus served on a half-cocked
Shell Oil sign:
                 what happened to the hairline between
luck and fingerluck, faint and fingerpaint, real hate
and masturbate? The ancient ensign of fertility becomes
an oil-slick Shell of itself rigged out in a Union
lawsuit suffocating seals through channels off the shores
of Santa Barbara; (but it doesn't matter:
                         the official
seals have lost their patron saint since the spinster, Paul,
namesake of the sterile nut who preached at Ephesus and
transformed the glory of sex into a neon glare,
ecstasy into the gift of tongues, the miracle
of cunnilingus, conversion of the Jews into
a catatonic stare, epiphany into a museum piece,
demoted Barbara from the symphony of tourist sites.
To wit:
             Paul the compassionate, the rhythm-method man,
the lewd little monk condemning his flock to
dementia praycocks by the calendar, to studying
the calendar like whoroscopes for some sign of safety from
female eggs in the frying phase; this programmed
Paul it was who stripped Barbara's sleeves
of their Chevron Oil aces and created one less "safe"

day in the calendar of saints, one more dangerous hole
card to be counted in the studs poker score, counted
with a straight face by those countering the feudal
graffiti forms of fertility with the distiller's
coil and pill-sought, drunken stare. For MIRV
Griffin is an acronym for commonplace America, many
warheaded monster sprung from dwarfed Minutemen;
Concord farmers protecting corncribs have
become corrupt from soil bank corn squeezins, drunk
with power and sterile from filling silos with missile
phalluses instead of seed. . . .)
                        Remembering all
this, savagely I raked the shorn grass and piled
it onto the heap of dead leaves and branches; then
I cut the fresh cowlicks down and trimmed
the mustaches here and there, plucked the lawn's
eyebrows and shaved its hairy neck and snipped
the wild hairs out of its nostrils and ears:
                                I slicked
down its hair and shook out the hairy sheet
and asked my son to agree that the job was done.
He nodded and we both stepped back to survey
the starkened scene and were satisfied. . . .
                                   Then
the chill of dusk stopped the running sweat
on my back and made me shiver; like a leaf on a shaking
limb, the child shivered too, grafted his hand
in mine. The stench of blood steamed above
the lawn, although sunshine had cauterized billions of bleed-
    ing
blades. Dew fell, soothing the stiffening scabs.
I shook myself, savage with reverie and resenting
the sterile-looking lawn, and turned to the rubbish heap
with hate. I sprinkled some gasoline—a libation
of the lawn mower's own blood—onto the leaves and grass
to get a good start, and then I set the blaze. Long
into the night, the wet grass smoldered and flared

as it dried; long we stared—animal-eyed,
entranced by the same mystique, a bloodlust beyond
the mere symbiosis of father and son—into
the boneless blaze, the rock-fed, hell-framed signal fires.
And then I took a bath and went to bed.

For a long time I wallowed and soaked, baptizing the water
with ingrained dirt, trying to steam out the stench
of blood and the sting of smoke; I rubbed myself pink,
as a start, at the finish, and, naked, then pierced
the darkness into the master's bedroom with a glowing
skin. Standing in the doorway, my eyes calibrating
to the gloom cast by moonlight through the open
window beside the bed and the night light—fallen,
comet-flake of phosphorescence—near the floor. Feverish,
I shivered with a chill but stifled a flash—a bulletin
hot from my balls predicting menopause, death
to all notions conceived beyond skin—urging
me to press under the covers instantly,
offset my feelings with front page pronouncements, headline
my heartache with hot lead linotype:
                                    my dreamlife lay
on the sheets stretched like a printing press waiting to
        be enrolled
in ink, typeset in duplicity,
schooled at duplicating a five-star finale
in fetal form:
                    the chasely turned-down bed,
soil banked with rolling silos like pillows and pubic
mosquito pits, booby trapped by buttocks and breasts
decolleté with dividends, ecology divided by safe
boxes deposited full of poison and LSD lust, self
interest rates, so the weed-rimmed driveways reminded me
of the lawn just mown, and that conception rutted
me back to my old routine:
                        I readied the bed
in a roundabout way, using the standard oil of romantic

reconnaissance, i.e., first raping out the rocks that might
give the mind bends, drowning it in robber-barren trends,
or snap the whirling propellor blades powering
the drilling rig we rode; then raking up the dead leaves
and sticks and heaping them all into a pile on the moonlit
reef, the surf-wracked floor beside the bed:
    and then I threw the clutch in gear and began to mow
easily, without thought or passion, in straight wide
sweeps, methodically, calculated to get the job
done in the least amount of time, grass spurting
in an arc from the side exhaust like spray from the bow
of a motorboat. Time itself had taught me the value
of time, and now my biological clocks
were gearstripped. With the automatic pilot on and the child
asleep and out of danger in the room next-door,
there was nothing to do but sit and steer. (As if
danger had anything to do with space or time,
instead of flight plans synchronizing to consciousness.)
Slowly, the stench of burning leaves and wet grass
seeped into the room, and for a long, long time before
escaping into sleep—synchromeshing dreams
and stripped desire—I stared into the soft, smoldering
embers of what had been a bonfire set
in the center of my concrete drive. . . . The weeds will
come back in another week, I thought, and wouldn't it
be marvelous just to let them grow wild? But what
would the neighbors think? In the end, the loaves and fishes
were just loaves and fishes and miracles would not spring
from fragments, smoldering debris; for milk-and-honey
modern man was breast-, and not wild locust-fed.

Quincy's
California
First Communion

He had seen the room a million times before; this was
only a slicker, more expensive version: the inevitable TV set,
inevitably clamped to the wall to baffle theft; the inevitable
writing table decorated with the inevitable monogrammed
ash tray and book of matches; the inevitable sterilized bathroom replete with a plastic bucket for hangover ice (down
the hall to the ice machine: twenty-five cents a scoop), and
a bottle opener socketed to the wall beside the waist-to-
ceiling bathroom mirror. The whole scene was laid for a
quick lay . . . even to the strategic hot plate available for
making instant coffee . . . dressed out in tinfoil packets. . . .
He didn't care. He was in California, and all he needed was
some sleep. In the morning, it would all look different, he
was sure. . . . The endless driving was a nightmare . . . but
he had made it, finally. . . . He collapsed on the bed fully

clothed and dropped into a drugged sleep. He was sure that if he opened the drawer of the night table, he would find a Gideon Bible inside. . . .

When he woke, he was deep in dark and starved. He showered off the road grime and quickly dressed. It was almost midnight and he wanted to get some food before the motel restaurant closed. If he hurried, he might still be able to manage something . . . might still be able to see something of the town. . . .

The candle-lit dining room was closed, but the hospital-stark snack bar was not: after a hamburger and chocolate shake, he strolled into the bar and had a drink. The soul sister at the piano was trying to get the sound of cotton fields into her song, but her mouth was too cottony from cigarettes, her tongue too tanned from alcohol, her back too fat from too many indifferent lovings on too many spiderdown bedsprings. She didn't have sense enough to feign complacence about her so-called suffering, to say she was lazy because she didn't care, was past pretending about the meaning of right and wrong: too much suffering can make you be a bore. He listened but let his mind go limp: the bourbon mellowed in his mouth before each lazy swallow and he drifted in the soothing dark. She should have been trying to say that confessing hypocrisy was not pretense; maybe it was the only way to be sincere. He listened and almost fell asleep. . . . Maybe he had: the waitress was asking if he wanted a refill before they had to close. He shook his head and rose to leave: he had the uncanny feeling he was still sleeping in his room. . . . Sound from the soft piano lay under the ceiling like layers of frozen smoke; dim light was pocketed in pools across the floor. When he left, drifting with the soft corks of sound bobbing to the surface from coral-reef piano keys, he splashed through the puddles of light across the floor, tight-rope-walked the flagstones of light to the barroom door, heading for the men's room and a little stroll: he wanted to savor the feeling of being free, the sense of fulfillment he associated with being in California—a dream come true at last! Behind him, the eddies he created in the pools of sound by departing died, widened to the walls and disappeared. . . .

He visited the men's room and defecated for the first time in the state of California: the only thing different about it was the size of his deposit, naturally, since he had been accumulating waste since dawn, had refused to stop in his anxiety to make San Diego without delay. Still bemused—no doubt still suffering from the kind of hypnosis that happens on long trips, staring at the open road and sun so long—he decided to take a stroll. His mellow mood must be fatigue, he thought, the letdown of having made it, the slackening tension that accompanies surrender. . . .

He followed the exit signs down a carpeted corridor, and, through a glass door, he emerged in a long arcade. He strolled inside the arches for a while, glancing indifferently at the darkened surface of shop windows along the way: reflected moonlight cast a silver sheen on the sheet-glass surfaces. The arcade was deserted: down a short flight of steps and he stepped out onto the lawn. The lawn was dotted with beach chairs and a stray blanket or two forgotten at the close of day; this night was not the debris of day, however; it seemed whole and fully sure. The moon was white as milk and as full as a nursing breast: it shone like a paten in the sky. A long row of torches—looking like saucers of flame suspended in midair—burned on the far side of the swimming pool and in a line parallel to the farther side. The torches reminded him of floating magic carpets, votive candles suspended in a seance, of torches held aloft by invisible fishermen embarked on midnight expeditions with a spear. He strolled over to the pool and stretched out on a chaise longue on the terrazzo apron which ringed the pool. How quiet and peaceful here! The turf had felt so thick and spongy, even through his shoes. He'd like to grip it with his toes. The music from the piano bar was a distant blur; occasionally, above the music from the bar, the note of a car's horn on Highway 80 would merge with the night sounds of insects, the chirping of crickets, the random pulsing of

fireflies. . . . Oh, how sweet and still! After so much roaring
wind and sun, this was sweet relief! He was drifting off to
sleep. . . . Is peace the meaning of being free? His face and
eyelids burned from so much sun; when he closed his eyes,
he could still visualize the glaring roads. . . . The pool,
lighted from within, glowed an eerie green. . . . The pool
was divided into racing lanes by black lines along the bottom; beneath the gently waving water, the black lines looked
like wavering lightning streaks.

He kept himself very still, breathing carefully. A figure—
spectral at first and tinged on the flanks and shoulders with
floating torchlight—detached itself from the darkness under
the torches and came to the far side of the swimming pool.
As she approached, she seemed to be a white face and shoulders moving in suspension above a pair of long and silver
legs; when she paused at poolside to put on her swimming
cap, he realized why: she was wearing a black, one-piece
bathing suit that had blacked-out her middle and blended
with the night. And now, after bending her head to brood
over the brink of the pool for a moment, she lowered herself
into the water and slipped beneath the surface without a
sound. He watched her swimming under water—in smooth
breast strokes—and wondered if he had been seen. Now this
was something different! Her body wavered beneath the
water like the long black racing lines. She surfaced opposite
where he sat and swam, soundlessly, in long smooth strokes,
to the shallow end of the pool on his right. Trying not to
lift his head for fear of being seen, he strained to see where
she was now. Soundlessly, she was swimming back, retracing
her wake in a controlled crawl: she seemed to be sliding over
emerald glass. Like random asteroids, like meteorites doomed to live for a day, fireflies blinked and circled the saucers
of floating flame: satellites to flying saucers, he thought and
almost laughed out loud—but he was afraid that she would
hear. Sounds from the distant bar and highway made soft
music for this watery ballet: floating on the water, she was
levitated like the torches' flames.

Suddenly the music stopped and the light inside the pool snapped off: the party's over and the bar was closed. He held his breath and stayed very still. He had enjoyed, been touched by the breath of beauty, and now he would wait for her to leave and go to bed. For the first time in a long time he almost felt content. The moon bulged like an aching breast; the shine on his face was fierce. Now the face of the swimming pool was black, and red light from the torches reflected from its blackened skin: the torchlight shimmered and wavered feverishly. The moon, like a white communion wafer, undulated in the center of the pool.

And suddenly she was beside him, breathing easily. She sat on the grass beside his chair, facing him at his feet. Her wet hair hung to her waist in straight black lines; the right side of her face was lined with a silver sheen. "The water is wonderful," she said; "so warm and yet so cool." She took his hand and held it, stroking it in the dark. And as they sat listening to the silence, hearing the torches hiss and flare, he remembered the different women in the motel piano bar, the old bags trying to excite desire by remembering what desire had been; the young ones trying to cool their aging escorts by pretending to forget—pretending that melting hot Scotch rocks were classy because they carried a money clip . . . and he remembered the couples dawdling over drinks trying to forestall the inevitable, the boredom of bedding down, afraid to admit they were bored with the bedding and hoped that a change of sheets or skins would make something different, although—with another drink, perhaps—it was difficult to see how or why, now that all the old positions had been tried—and re-tried—lo, these many moons ago. . . .

"Like to try it?" she asked him softly and leaned forward to kiss his fingertips. Specks of moonlight shone in her liquid eyes. When she blinked, it was like fireflies flashing in the dark. Her hair was a tented cape around her shoulders; moonlight shone in her pitch-black hair.

"I don't have a bathing suit," he said, entranced. Her pupils were shaped like tiny candle flames: they burned with a steady, cat-like intensity. He felt hypnotized.

"Don't be silly," she said and smiled quietly, afraid to break the spell. The surface of the pool was silver, shot through with marble streaks of red light from the flaring torches. And then she stood and knelt beside him, facing the pool, offering him her back. "Unzip," she said and bowed her head and hunched her shoulders up.

With trembling fingers, he parted her hair into a wedge aimed at the bottom of her neck: he took a deep breath as if preparing for a dive and unzipped her bathing suit with a long, smooth stroke. The incision was firm and clean: her tight suit curled open from the top, the black suit parting like a tight skin and shrinking from a slash. Turning to face him she stood and slipped out of her wet suit and dropped it, a shapeless mass, soaking at her feet, drying, like an abortion, in the grass. Then she stroked her body from breasts to thighs, skinning off the excess water, and then she stood on tiptoe and stretched her arms up to the sky. For a moment, the moon was a silver beach ball balanced between her fingertips: then she lowered her arms and backed away, beckoning, urging him to join her in the pool. "I'll be waiting, so hurry," she whispered, and, turning away in a slow-motion pirouette that seemed to be shaped in smoke, she faded away in the moonlight and slipped into the water.

I'm ashamed, he said to himself and shivered: he sat up and strained to see her in the pool, but he could not. Either she was beneath the surface, or moonlight was not enough to see her by, he thought. If he wanted her, he would have to go. The surface of the water was shattered with streaks of light.

He was ashamed of feeling shame. Wasn't this California, where things were different? And wasn't he now free? He slipped out of his clothes, and, forcing himself to do it slowly, strode upright to the pool. For a long moment, he posed at poolside, his face lifted to the moon; then he slipped into the water. He shed his shame as he slipped beneath the shallow waves. . . .

For the longest time he could imagine, as long as interstellar space flight, as long as a fetal dream, they swam together in the darkened pool, side by side in long solemn strokes, plunging and surfacing like dolphins, locked in airtight kisses, arms and legs locked in death grips, they rolled over and over in silver-blackened water as if suspended beyond gravity in airless space and time. How long is a dream without gravity? Some things you have to take on faith, he thought; but he wanted to affirm his life: to do that, life itself must be affirmed.

Breathless, weary but not released from all the roiling, hand in hand, they waded to the shallow part of the pool. And now they stood face-to-face, his back against the side of the hollow square: her breasts seemed suspended between them, floating in a black half-brassiere. He kissed her, pressing back against the pool's side, feeling streams of tiny bubbles tingling up his legs and sides, almost listening to hear them pop as they broke the surface: the water had settled into moon-soldered silence before he broke their kiss gently and drew himself over the edge of the pool and sat, legs apart, staring down into her moon-white face. Her face floated on the surface like a water lily nestled in a hair-nest lily pad. The silence of eternal peace, of timeless dream, floated in her lily face and sealed the waters into sleep. And black champagne bubbles sizzled along her legs. Till suddenly the torches flared, hissed like gas jets and expired: the flames disappeared as if sucked back into the torches' tall supporting stems. Now night was completely dark except for the blazing moon, which, relieved of the contrast with earthly light, now shone brighter than before.

Slowly, moving through the water without a ripple, she stepped between his open legs and grasped his knees: her lifted face was molded in moonlight before she closed her eyes and lowered her face into his lap. She cupped her hand under her chin like a communion plate: to lose a single crumb was sacrilege. He lay back on the pool's apron, his knees bent over the edge, his feet rooted in water. His sex pointed like a periscope, and, although he stared straight into the blazing moon, he failed to see. For she blinded his periscope, submerging it under wildly lapping waves, holding it under until—his spasming legs stiffening under her armpits and lifting her from the water—the spurting torpedoes exploded on target. When the periscope surfaced again its blindness was aggravated by a spineless limp. And the limp was the feat of a chronic cripple; it always recurred.

She flushed her face in the shimmering water and drew up beside him: for a long while they rested, lying on their backs side by side on the terrazzo apron, staring moonstruck into the mirror sky. A dark stain of wetness—solid as a shadow—merged and widened around their bodies. A dense cloud, a cloud with well-defined but ragged edges, drifted over the face of the brilliant moon. For a moment, the moon looked as if its bottom had been eaten out; but then the cloud blew away and the moon reappeared, whole and clear once more. He felt as if his soul had been sucked out through a straw, but after the cloud had crossed the face of the staring moon, they rose and silently paced hand in hand into the deeper shadows of the turf. Within reach of the row of quenched torches, he pulled her to the spongy turf and tied her into a love knot, their arms and legs tangled like pythons in a death grip. Savagely, brutally, in quick succession—without bothering (perhaps unable) to uncouple between spurts—they loved one another, in a rhythm of snarls, in a tempo of sweet obscenity: they wrestled for release without finding it completely, until, exhausted, side by side they fell asleep. . . .

When he woke again the moon had waned into the depths of night: he was exhausted but fully clothed and stretched out on the chaise longue beside the swimming pool. His legs trembled when he stood. Holding his head high like a blind man, and probing the darkness before his face with flickering fingertips, he found his way through the remaining night, down the dim corridors of the plush motel, back to his room and fell into a drugged sleep without bothering to undress.

How long he slept, he did not know. But when he sat bolt upright in bed, it was still pitch dark inside his room. Trembling from a blind, irrational fear, he forced himself to grope his way to the window and open the Venetian blinds. High on a hilltop—diminished by distance, but toy-stark and clear nonetheless, almost exactly opposite his window on the other side of Highway 80 and far away—stood a white belfry bathed in magenta light. The reddish glow seeped downward in the darkness like a heavy fog; white buildings clustered under and near the belfry were also touched with the swirling light. But perched on its blacked-out hilltop, the belfry seemed disembodied, suspended in midair with only the powdery light for roots. Quincy stared at the mirage-like image for a long time, puzzled by why it had awakened him—for he was convinced that, in some mysterious way it *had,* succubus-like, invaded his sleep and aroused him with a start—he was puzzled about *why* the spotlighted belfry should bother him. It was a lighthouse, a beacon light, a means and image of security: why should that bother him? He was saturated with a sense of guilt, stuttering with shame. Fearfully, he crept back to a night of fitful sleep. Maybe things were the same in California, after all.

The next day, he strode through the motel swiftly and immediately to the swimming pool; she was not there, of course. In fact, however, for all he knew, she might have been; he wasn't sure he'd remember her now, even if she were: in daylight, everything seemed so different. Nevertheless, to the best of his recollection, he retraced the route he had followed last night—the route he *thought* he followed, he said to himself—and what *was* the best of his recollection? I must have been punch-drunk from all that driving, he thought and slipped into the chaise longue by the swimming pool. It was the same all right, he said to himself and relaxed: he squirmed until he adjusted to the stinging heat from the plastic-covered cushions. Finally, the sting went away and he was adjusted to the sun. The water in the pool was blue: the westering sun on its surface was blistering in brilliance, baffled and stung his eyes with a bouncing glare. The lawn was littered with loungers and bathers cultivating cancer cells on their slug-like skins; children splashed and squealed; parents shrugged and pretended to be happy watching their offspring in delight, enjoying themselves cavorting like spirochetes, sperm cells splashing in the chlorinated womb; bathing beauties preened and promenaded, tanning quickly under the stares of big-breasted, paunchy middle-aged men. The surface of the swimming pool stung his eyes: he tried to peer into its depths, but its surface was impenetrable: my angle of vision is probably too low, he thought, too close to the water line. The surface flashed and stung as if the facet of each wave, the splinters of each splash, were fragments of a mirror throwing up the sun. He lifted his eyes for relief to the high diving board.

She was facing west with the setting sun full upon her face, but she did not flinch. When she reached the top of the tall ladder, she paused and drew herself up to her full height. The dying sun lighted her golden hair into a copper glow. With her arms at her sides, she pulled up to tiptoe and her deeply tanned body became taut. In her red bathing suit, her hair seemed the flame of a human torch: her body was the flame of the torch-like diving tower. . . .

In a timing of dream-like slow motion, the precision that comes of long practice, she paced to the end of the diving board, thrust her paralleled arms straight above her head and drew up her right knee and bounced on the springy board. Effortlessly, she soared into the air, and, at the peak of her swan dive, she reminded him of the figurehead of a clipper ship, a boomerang, as sleek and taut-breasted as a filled spinnaker: she struck the water with a clean, sharp splash. Time after time, tirelessly, she repeated her dive: he was fascinated. What splendor and what grace! He was getting a hard-on: this was real all right! He felt embarrassed and crossed his legs and tried to hide it: guiltily he looked around. There were times when the stupid thing seemed to have a mind of its very own, goddammit! But no one seemed to notice; in fact, he started to wish that she *would* see. The paunchy men stared at her too behind their sunglasses, pretending to drowse, however, as their flabby wives dozed, wishing they could dream. . . . On the far side of the swimming pool, the gas-fed torches which had acolyted the communion scene last night were dead: the torches were tall black sticks topped with brass saucer-shaped fittings; they looked like empty candle sticks. Squinting, he scoured the lawn behind the swimming pool, especially the area beneath the torches where they had lain. . . . Nothing.

Suddenly she was beside him, sauntering by slowly, on her way into the motel, to shower and dress for dinner. She materialized out of the flashing glare of the swimming pool—like grunion mating on the beach between two wave beats—and she was gone. He blinked from sun blindness, almost unable to believe that she was real. Hurry, hurry! Before she gets away!

"Hey, baby, that's real Olympic form," he said, trying to sound tough and nonchalant. It wasn't his idiom, but this was California, the home of movies and hippiedom, and he hoped that the idiom of make-believe might be real for this situation.

It was hardly a pause and her eyelashes hardly flickered: one leg barely slowed in its steady stride and her eyes barely tilted towards the sound—but it was a practiced eye, for predators learn to make quick appraisals since it's a question of survival—and a glance as quick as instinct told her all that she had to know. Her first reaction was cool indifference rather than contempt; next, her heart skipped a beat. My God, how blond and beautiful he was! And not some wise-cracking kid or cigar-smelling, middle-aged cheater for a change! And then his crotch caught her eye and the smile which had started to flicker on her face froze: hardly breaking stride, she swept on by. She thought she kept her face straight; Quincy was shriveled by contempt. He crossed his legs and lay very still. He closed his eyes against the glaring sun. The endlessly blue sky was getting on his nerves. It was like being in a prison cell where they never shut off the ceiling light, where you had the feeling of round-the-clock surveillance.

He lay very still, feeling his face burn, listening to the splashes fading in the failing sun, the squeals and laughter of the children fade, and cigar smoke clear away on a breeze from the open sea. . . . As the cushions on the chaise longue cooled, he fell asleep.

When he woke, the swimming pool was deserted; its surface was dull and grey. The sun was setting and it was starting to get dark: the sky was the color of sharkskin and the lighted torches on the other side of the pool danced dimly: the flames were pink and pale.

He rose stiffly, as if his bones had congealed like cooling lard, as if the unexpended sperm of his hard-on had receded from his sacs and spread throughout his system and stiffened as he cooled, the blood of his hard-on spreading into body-wide rigor mortis. That's what comes of frustration, he told himself and stretched. Smiling, he strode into the motel stiffly, warming gradually as he walked. Well, you can't win 'em all, he said to himself as he checked out. He might have stayed an extra night—for dinner, anyway; but now he was anxious to get away. He didn't want to risk seeing the blonde again. Only five o'clock, he thought; still time to find myself a place.

He bought a paper in the lobby, intending to study the classifieds for a place to rent, but he decided on a better plan. Since he didn't know the city anyway, he figured he'd just "cruise": homeless, the method had served him in the past. . . .

When he left the motel parking lot, he stashed his luggage in the trunk and pulled away, careful to keep his eyes at sea level: he didn't want to see the belfry hovering high on the hill on the other side of the highway, magenta light or not.

Wings

    The wings, ah, the wings are the last to go, I thought,
as I mounted the sterile stairs into the upper
reaches of this classroom building of a college for blacks—
a hospital campus splinted together like a collage
of hate-filled history, desperation and starved
desire, *ah, the wings, the wings are the last to go,*
I thought, and struggled up the stairs, straining for breath,
as I mounted through atmospheres of racial memory,
    reached
into regions where the air was thinned by mythic flights
and fear, ancestral rages and loves enriched
in the lungs of memory by Jung, *ah, the wings, the wings*
are the last to go, I thought, and sought to climb
above the storm into understanding and starved my blood
    instead,
climbing—pitons, precipices, handholds and alpenstocks,

stabbed into the heart of struggle, and cold, numbing
movement and glacial wind—warring against *wings,*
ah, the wings are the last to go, I reminded myself
as I struggled upward to understand, and,
try as I might, accomplished self-satisfied suicide
instead, for my upward thrust was reacted by a downward
pull, gravity that bled blood from my brain
to overweight my toes: *ah, the wings, the wings are the last*
to go! What was I climbing to, up these sterile
stairs? What apogee of knowledge achieve, I could not
achieve at levels with the ground? Breathless—blacked out
like a test pilot in a power dive—my brain would not
understand: I doubt if my toes—swollen to
elephantiasis-size by clots of unwormed
blood—could understand the earth they came down to
by themselves and fallen from arches cornerstoned
in the vault of my skull: *ah, the wings, the wings are the last*
to go! Yet a "racial memory"? As in/from an atavistic
dream of flight, an unlearned nisus that impels
me to build my nest, implant my seed, detonate
myself to death with depth charges launched in pursuit
of sex, the stalking sub of the wolf pack fixed
like a crooked fight, programmed to finish by a knockout
in a tank town? death timed by a bell rigged
to biological clocks and DNA molecules instead
of your puny will? Ah, the wings, the mythic
wings! Determined to savage love and hate?
And was that the clue—purblind desire—the answer
to the failure I climbed to now, wondering what parachute
I might use when I finally accepted my ceiling of failure
and was jettisoned into thinking I had to jump, bail
out of bondage I was flying blind on a Kamikaze flight?
Was death the only way to jump bail? Was life
merely the future forfeit to law? What
have I forgotten when my racial memory
reminds me of my rotted wings disintegrated by
the fierce device of a frowning father, an instinct

as deep as Daedalus and searing as the sun? I shrugged
and mounted to my class, climbing the stairway I had
to go. Upwards I climbed, retracing the squarely
rooted tiers of evolution, around and around,
upward through the past, spiraling into the solid
geometry of syntax, the hologram of language illuming
the human mind, a skeleton of shadows, the spinal mush
that keeps the soul alive, the 3-D mirage of matter
and uniform we call the mind lasered in language
that looks so linear *because ah, the wings, the wings! can
sunlight sustain a vacuum? can wings assault
and sail through empty space?* we move in self-created,
mind-concocted time? time measured in spatial molds,
cobblestoned into ice cubes, square-rooted fiction we call
the past, and freeways to the future? (The penis is an airport
runway into freedom, launching site of semen, spurt
of purpose raised to a higher power, a res-erected thing
that finds its freedom imprisoned as a fetus—timed
for parole as the exponent of a higher power still?)
Ah, the wings, the blindly drunken wings! My job
was Freshman Comp and Lit., autogyroed language
and mind interchangeable, one for the other and
neither possible without the same, for what we learn is
the only thing possible for us to know, inherited
as a gift of tongues, bestowed like a time bomb, determined
to detonate against détente. *And when I say nigger,
Negro, black; and when I say guinea, shyster,
wop, I'm polluting the air that lifts my wings?*
And when I say grammar, syntax and spelling; and when
I say paragraph, organize, time, I'm
spacing the air to lift those wings, polluting
young minds with the muddle, beginning and end
of syllogistic time, pinning Aristotle's uniform feathers
on hairless wings? Or, trapped in a smog I cannot
escape, polluted air I must breathe to live,
transmit what I must as the only thing I know,
communicate disease since I cannot clean the surgeon's

knife? Thus I kill with the instrument I cannot cleanse,
since I too inherit what I must bequeath, kill
through the process I cannot clean. (The tubercular
giving mouth-to-mouth respiration might be more merciful
if he used a gun instead of sex.) But
teaching is talk and so I climb to my class, spraying
the air with the germ warfare of words, despite
the germ mask I wrap around my mind. *Ah, the wings, the glorious*
wings, are the last to go!, I cry to myself,
but find myself wondering . . . if any of my students really
cares?—self-pity aside, just do your job—
but can I reach them, if they have been immunized
against my breed of germs, the disease of language
I'm here to spread? Hate, dialect and street-life,
innoculates life from life, mind from mind,
and makes me wonder about those wings and the height
of the walls they must surmount, the temperature at which
they will melt, and whether a poisoned mind can find—
and use—an antidote against itself.
Society is smallpox: how much is enough
to make one immune? How much is
an overdose that kills the wings, ah, the wings?
I reached the landing and saw them once again,
lying on the ledge and shimmering in the sun, streaked
with lavender and stirred to life by a vagrant wind,
an echo of its deepening death, down stirring like
eyelids REMming in restless sleep, boning
blood losing its memory of life and settling
into the silt of itself, dimming memory of
its own dream of death. Death is amnesia, a sleep
walk with worms, awakening to a leper's loss
of eroded locomotion: coughing, the absent-minded
professor awakes in his coffin to find that
the trapeze-tightrope between life and death had
disappeared: he had nothing to teach but the way to walk,
and that should be shown—but the way was a sham. For

the way was a tightrope, a penile levitation between
two sterile points of time called past and future
suspended across the pit of present tense: choices
exist if you're doomed to go: follow the rope
or fall . . . into death, remembering its own decay
as life . . . recalling its birth as a flashback into
death. . . . Now on the landing I stopped to look,
as I had done for, lo, these many days.
At the bird I looked, dead on the ledge outside
the one-way window, as I paused on the landing to catch
my breath. For weeks I had been keeping a watch
this way, since the day in early fall when first
I noticed death emptying into its timeless
shape on the ledge outside the tinted, one-way
window that soared like a blue shaft up the side of the
    building
and blended into the TV antenna, the cobweb
of crucifixion electrocuting the modern mind,
towering above the roof it topped, masting
the deep like a modern sail, a ship of state
being steered by a talking sieve. But one day as
I paused on this poop-deck landing to catch my breath,
and leaned my brow against the glass, hoping
to cool my head with an overview by glancing into
the street, I saw the dead bird and the yellow ball-point
pen lying by its side. The ledge it lay
upon was a square canopy for the entrance far
below, a balcony as flat as a fireman's net
jutting out from the wall as if to catch
those who might jump— At any rate, it had caught
the bird. And the bird was as dead as a calling card
served on a salver. Where had it fallen from? I twisted
upward, pressed against the glass, but could not see.
Dizzy, I pulled back. For a moment, I felt
as if I might melt through the window and plunge to the
    pavement
far below. . . . I caught my breath by lifting my eyes

to the treeline in the distance and telling myself that vertigo,
like images of time, was a rapture of self-deceit,
a trap the past had lain for the future reflecting self
defeat.
     Steady now, I stood above the bird
and stared, watching through the window and remembering
    banks
of babies deposited in incubators and bassinets behind
a sterilizing shield of glass (toasting burnt-out
time is money, multiplying as fast as foreclosed
human flesh), and a nurse—smiling behind
a germ mask like a genial robber arrived to run
an audit with a revolver loaded for Russian roulette—
holding up a bundled blob for me to see,
assuring me that the toast she was raising—the buttered
slice of my life beneath the blanket—was indeed
my son, still wet from the mint as half-baked dough,
filling his rompers with runs on the dirty bank. . . . Once
    more
I looked at the bird on its back, and after that,
I turned away. Its tiny feet were tucked
up tight in a fetal tension under its tail.
(I remember how, when my son was born, they had
to pry his limbs apart, peel him open like a raw
banana, shake him open like a sheathed umbrella,
so much time had he spent in his spaceship, cramped
into the weightless surfaces of a launching site, awaiting
his orbital release into long parole: life
is merely death on a leash, a dog lashed
to death, a shortening leash circling the sun.
Time is tethered to the center of space—me.)
How big was the bird? A few inches, no more—smaller
than a sparrow—and blue-gray in color, changing in the sun-
    light
like a dolphin drying on the deck. Its belly and the inside
of its wings shimmered—lavender, red and gold—
like a rainbow-oil slick in a wet dirty street. Its wings

were slack and its head turned limp, hung black against
the canopy of stone. Fully feathered, it could not have
    bombed
from a nest high above; more likely, it had
smashed into the one-way window and broken its neck.
(People frequently forget and try to walk through
glass doors—fall through rabbit holes, read the future
in the names men drop, merds of the human mind—so why
shouldn't birds? And who's to say what kind of walking
water will or will not support?)
                                I couldn't
look any more and turned away, climbed
upward to my class, embarrassed by the bustle around
me in the hall, drowning me on the diving-
float landing, catching Dracula out of his cocoon during
a change in classes commiserating a stupid dead
bird. But for days, weeks, months after that,
I watched the progress of decay: each day
as I struggled up the stairs, straining to achieve some
understanding, I always paused at the landing to catch
my breath and stare at the decomposing bird,
measure the wind and weather, the snow and rain,
doing their stealthy, savage work. After
a while, I ceased to care who was watching me—
let them smile or laugh, I thought, ignoring
them as they jostled past, on their way
to or from class, answering the beckon of a different
bell: why should I mind who was watching me,
since the bird—defenseless, naked in death—was not
embarrassed by me watching *it?* I was sure I was learning
more than they as I watched the ants scoop out
the tiny carcass, watched sun strip the tiny
bones and wind whip the rootless feathers far
away, until *ah, the wings, neither head nor heart,*
are the last to go! until the carcass was brittle and dry,
and, if I listened closely, could seem to hear
it scrape and crackle like a dry leaf through the glass.

Bloodlines

After weeks, there was little left but the burnished wings,
shined and blackened by the winter sun, awry
and barely joined by a webbing of backbone and tiny
rotting ribs. Once, for weeks, the pen
and wings were buried under snow: there was barely a
    swelling,
a white welt, to show where the wings had been.
Still I paused to see—at least kept watch—for when
the wings should reappear, rust through
the primer coat of snowpaint purity. The wings
could not be winterized against rust and rot:
Prestone could not stop—snow nor
formaldehyde—petrifying bones from
thawing marrow into mush. But
I was withering with worry—worry about the problem
of being white, white in a black school—
and the difficulty of crossing the color-line of skin and life-
    style,
mixbreeding psychosis and history, into higher—any—
plane of communication, contact, region of response
where words were not the wound of one hand clapping,
were not heartbeats hiccuping mea culpas,
were wings clapping the sounds of syphilis against
a solid side and causing the bird to rise
and fly like a fish to the lure of dirty sex, dive
deep into the polluted stream, infected
life force. Clap, clap, clap—but
it didn't seem to work. Flying was as painful as passing
bloody piss. All I was raising—"popular"
or not—was clouds of eraser dust and doubt.
I wanted more—much more: to prove that brotherly
love was possible—beyond toleration, more
than passive ripples overriding my paleface presence, than
the tokenism that white teachers here meant integration,
compliance with guidelines set by the state against
bile welling in my guts. . . . Skin, I was discovering,
was the color-line of words and just as hard to penetrate,

get across to get to the meaning of . . . sex. . . . They say
I can't understand their psyche because they're black:
is not a wop white? is not a Jew black? has not
the leper felt the same lash? *Ah, the wings, the wings
are the last to go!* Why should they know *me,* if I
not *them?* . . .
      In the depth of winter, a student startled
me on the stairs. In fact, I was on the landing,
staring at the snow, trying to see beneath the surface
to the buried bird. "Say," he said, "watch you
all uptight about? Give it time, give it time."
I looked at him and smiled. His Afro, mustache
and dark glasses didn't faze me any more. I thought
I understood. "Dig, man," he said, "I'm an existentialist,
see? I mean, das cool. You dig? I mean,
I'm *me,* an' you is *you,* an' we each is stuck in his own
tough skin. Alienation ain't a question of color, man.
You dig?" And then he winked and macked away. At least
I *think* he winked—I couldn't really tell, he was hiding
behind his shades, you see—but his cheek worked and he
    smiled:
"Keep cool," he said, as he waved his hand and pimped
away: keep cool. And suddenly, I smiled, too.
Why not? Keep cool, he said, and keep cool I did.
For suddenly I grasped the paradox of being understood,
of *understanding,* without meaning to, of being touched—
communicating, that timeless cliché—by someone talking
about alienation. Each was trapped in his own
tight skin, ok—nothing was settled, nothing
was solved—but the snowbank of worry melted and washed
away, melting money-words formed a puddle that drained
    away like piss,
that ran away like interest rates rising from inflation—
ah, the wings, the wings are the last to go! Now I turned
and climbed upward to my class, more trusting of my words.
For if luck is nothing, then nothing is luck; and if
love is trapped, then so is hate; and if

black is white, then white is black, and words
have a meaning turned on their backs. I smiled, walking
to my class, wondering if now I could find the words. . . .
They would have to be solid and down to earth: oh,
if only I could give them wings and still be believed!
  The snow froze and tightened into winter, crusting
over the carcass of the spellbound bird. But lean
winter light soon fattened into suety spring sun
and dripped grease-buds along all the branches
and softened the catatonic snow to slush and floes
swimming in the streets . . . the sewers gurgled and swirled
back to life, breeding bacteria and feeding
the fevers that thrive in spring. The frozen snow
embalming the bird thawed, and, bounding
up the steps one day, I remembered the bird and paused
for a peek instead of dashing past, on my way to more
useful work. The melting snow had
unpacked into a puddle, a little pond, in fact, swirling
down a drain to the left, a drain topped
by an onion-shaped filter of wires that reminded me
of a Moslemite mosque, and even as I watched—trying
to hear the water gurgle through the glass—the carcass
of the bird unstuck from the stone it had been frozen
to and rose slowly to the surface, floated
among the lesser ice floes and broke apart
as soon as it got caught in the current swirling down
the drain. The floating, slowly spinning wings reminded
me of a catamaran or an outrigger manned
by a Polynesian crew, the way the black, weathered wings
were bolted by a delicate webbing of vertebrae and fragile
bones that broke up in collision with the current and chunks
of swirling ice, the blundering bergs and caps of a lesser,
of a wingless world. . . . *Ah, the wings, the wings are the last*
to go! Is there something rock-bottom that separates black
and white? Is it psyche or is it sex? Is skin
the color of language, are words the palette that breeds
are mixed upon? Is skin as deep as one can go,

since color is everything? Is the difference esthetic—beauty
is truth . . . and black is beautiful . . . and all most need
to know is that what they like they see? As I watched,
the webbing between the wings broke apart, so that now
the wings were floating free, each a brittle canoe of its own,
a blade—a scimitar—stabbing into the current
and rocking toward the drain. The wings still looked
waterproof, black and slick as hard shellac,
but as they slammed into the filter they instantly broke
apart, stabbing like brittle knives, thrust
by the current against the cutting wires, the bloodless
wings broke and feathers scattered on the waters
like crumbled petals, dry leaves crushed to dust
and scattered in the stream. Heartbroken, I couldn't bear
to watch: what happened to my happiness, my springbok
    bounce
of a moment or so before? Now the ice
on the water looked like mold, like rinds of
leprous skin clinging to the murky water,
parasitic lily pads of rotting, putrid flesh. . . .
    When the water level dropped, however, I noticed
the yellow ball-point pen: yes, it was still
there, I thought, and even if it doesn't work
any more, if the ink is solid or watered out,
still, plastic won't decay so that something—a symbol,
at least—of the pen still survives. But I turned away
dissatisfied. Mounting slowly to my class, I thought,
symbol or not, what good is a pointless yellow
pen? I was faced again with the conflict as
before, the dividing line between surface and conception,
deceit and surface fact. *Ah, the wings, the wings—*
the wings are the last to go! I had achieved a rapport
with my students, an elbow-rubbing rapport, of sorts
(the sort that rubs my professional sweaters
into a sheen of skepticism at the elbow?); in short,
I had achieved disguised acceptance, truce
declared so untouchables could be treated with leper-tongs:

and I had understood—accepted—*them,* in a way—
but I wondered, sadly, if we simply hadn't adjusted
to each other, shark and pilot fish, mongoose and snake,
death and taxation, taxidermy with *nature mort,*
a marriage of convenience based on non-support,
a symbiosis of mutual mistrust. . . . Sadly,
as I passed the window a few days later, descending
from my last class for the day, I was startled to notice
that even the ball-point pen was gone! The ledge
looked clinical and clean in the late spring sun,
and not a shred of bird—wing or ball-point—was
to be seen! Incredible! Surely, the current could
not have been strong enough to flush the pen away?
It would have taken an eagle to cash and carry
it back as a beam in building his nest, and,
heaven knows, the eagle hasn't carried any credit in these
    parts
in years, if ever; in fact, the bird is practically
bankrupt throughout the world. I shrugged, and sadly
passed on. It was impossible but true: even the pen
had been floated and flushed down the drain. If I looked,
I might find it in the street or on the sidewalk far
below. But it didn't matter now, I thought, I haven't
got time to nurse death through another winter.
Life is too short, I thought, especially since
the wings, ah, the wings are the last to go! and they do,
they do, they do. . . .
                    In a minute, I was in the street,
trudging through the snowless, naked world. Why should
the world, so lush with new spring lies, seem barren
now? New life lurked everywhere I looked. . . .
In the street, I turned back to the classroom building I had
just left and sighted up the long shaft of colored
glass which sheered up the cliffside building: in
afternoon light, the glass was black and I wondered
how any bird could have blundered against it, broken
its neck against the mask in the iron man and leaded to the

ledge.
I quickly scanned the sky in search of skimming birds.
   Luckily,
there were none. In spite of spring, I heard no twittering
in the trees as I left the campus quickly, my eyes upon the
   ground. . . .
For alive or dead, when the new birds came again,
I thought, that's where they would be, if they returned
at all. . . . *Ah, the wings, the kiwi wings upon the ground,*
I thought, and, staring at the sun-washed world,
I began to wonder why *the wings, ah, the wings are the last
   to go!*